Idaho's Poetry

A Centennial Anthology

Edited by
**Ronald E. McFarland and
William Studebaker**
Introduction by
William Stafford

University of Idaho Press

Compilation copyright (c) 1988 by Ronald E.
McFarland and William Studebaker.
Introduction copyright (c) 1988 by William Stafford.
Poems throughout are reprinted with the kind
permission of those sources given in full in the
Acknowledgments.
Published in 1988 by the University of Idaho Press,
Moscow, Idaho 83843, with the gracious assistance of
the Idaho Centennial Commission.
Design by Melissa Rockwood

9 8 7 6 5 4 3 2

Library of Congress Cataloging-in-Publication Data

Idaho's poetry : a centennial anthology / edited by
    Ronald E. McFarland and William Studebaker ;
    introduction by William Stafford.
        ISBN 0-89301-128-2 (pbk.)
        1. American poetry—Idaho.   2. Idaho—
Poetry.   I. McFarland, Ronald E.   II. Studebaker,
William.
PS571.I2I24 1988   811′.008′09796—dc19
            88-27660

ISBN 0-89301-128-2

❧ Table of Contents

Preface   *xv*

Acknowledgments   *xix*

Introduction   *1*

    Time-Lapse Poetry, by William Stafford,   *1*

        Springs Near Hagerman,   2

        Coyote,   2

        Idaho, by Howard Horowitz,   *4*

Native Poems   *5*

    Introduction,   5

    Nez Perce,   7

      Medicine-Song of the Elk,   7

      The Bear Hunter,   8

      The Rock Wren and the Rattlesnake,   8

      Medicine Song,   9

      Death Chant,   9

      Wyakin Song from a Male Buffalo,   9

      Three Songs of Mad Coyote (Wyakin),   10

      Smohalla Speaks,   10

      Coyote and the Swallowing Monster,   11

      Origin of the Sweat House,   12

      Phil George

        Old Màn, The Sweat Lodge,   14

        Name Giveaway,   15

        Morning Beads,   15

        Call of the Flute,   16

    Shoshone-Bannock and Northern Paiute,   16

      Neither Spirit Nor Bird,   17

      Glyphs,   17

      Lament of a Man for His Son,   18

      The Grass on the Mountain,   19

      Rain Song,   19

      Aspen Song,   20

      The Craters of the Moon,   20

      Coyote and the Rock,   21

Dana Cassadore
The Tribal Artist, 22
Credence, 22
Coeur d'Alene, 23
Lake Coeur d'Alene, 23
The Little People, 24
Janet Campbell Hale
Backyard Swing, 25
Desmet, Idaho, March 1969, 26
Kutenai, 26
The Deluge, 26
Sweatbath Prayer, 27

The Pioneer Poets (1860–1900)　　　　29

Introduction, 29
"Log-Cabin"
*A New Year View of the World Inside
and Out,* 32
A.J.
Our Cabin on the Bar, 33
anon.
To M.V.E., 35
"Scottish Chief"
Poor Man, 36
"Pay Rock"
The Owyhee Miner's Lament, 37
"Darby"
The Rustic Miner, 38
G.E.B.
*The Wild Forget-Me-Nots of
Owyhee,* 39
Sarah Huckvale
Bear Lake, 40
George P. Wheeler
The 'Bad Man' from the Range, 41
anon.
The Candidate, 42
"Arion"
Advice to Beaux, 43
"Vaquero"
To "Sally Cactus", 44

anon.
>   *Country Girls,*   44

anon.
>   *A Bachelor's Growl,*   45

"Grey Eagle"
>   *Up Goes Idaho,*   47

George P. Wheeler
>   *Idaho Retrospective,*   48

Naomi McDonald Phelps
>   *A Mountain Idyl,*   50

Clarence E. Eddy
>   *Springtime in Idaho,*   51

H. F. Johnson
>   *The Israelite's Last Mule Ride,*   53
>   *Farewell to Idaho,*   55

Poets of a New State (1900–1940),   59

Introduction,   59

Vardis Fisher
>   *Dick Rowe,*   62
>   *Hank Radder,*   62
>   *Joe Hunter,*   63

Donald Burnie
>   *Eva Kelly,*   63
>   *Harry Gale,*   64
>   *Wild Moll,*   64

Ezra Pound
>   *Moeurs Contemporaines,*   64

Annie Pike Greenwood
>   *The Farmer's Wife and Her Poem,*   69
>   *As I Wear a Gown,*   69
>   *Definition of Love,*   70

Irene Welch Grissom
>   *Clearing Sagebrush,*   71

Janet Ellen Miller
>   *The Big Boss,*   72

Paul Croy
>   *The Riverpig,*   73

Ruth Bernice Mead
>   *Mountain Interlude,*   74

Keith Barrette
>   *Rural Etching,*   75

Yvor Winters
   Nocturne, 75
   The Journey, 76
Carol Ryrie Brink
   The Fairy Wife, 77
   Foggy Day at the Beach, 78
   Thoughts on Eating an Apple, 78
Jean Chalmers Donaldson
   Young Farm Wife, 79
   Back Street Autumn, 79
   Hollyhocks, 80
   Velvet Foil, 80
Forrest Anderson
   springboard as a waterfront cafe, 81
   definitions, 81
   vol fantasque, 82
Bess Foster Smith
   Country Store, 82
Norman Macleod
   Evening Above the Snake, 83
   Ring Around the Syringas, 84
Edna Gillespie
   Wall-Flower, 86
E. A. Brubacher
   Joe Weaver of Owyhee, 86
Amy Woodward Fisher
   Rain in Harvest, 87
Edith M. Roberts
   Idaho Potato Field, 88

The Third Generation (1940–1980)   89

Introduction, 89
Duane Ackerson
   Beforehand, 91
   Weathering, 91
James Ater
   mountain vigil, 92
James Brock
   The Growth of Mathematics, 93
   The Recognition of Beasts, 94

Ed Dorn
>   *Home on the Range, February, 1962,*   94
>   *Chronicle,*   95
Carolyn S. Foote
>   *Widow,*   96
>   *Reflections,*   97
Sudie Stuart Hager
>   *A Spider Web in a Rose Garden,*   97
Kenneth O. Hanson
>   *Montana,*   98
Jim Heynen
>   *Traveling through Idaho on Opening Day,*   99
>   *Sioux Center, Iowa,*   99
Bonnie Cochrane Hirsch
>   *Knighthood in Grangeville,*   101
>   *Me an Mason Williams, Down the*
>   *Garden Path,*   102
Jim Irons
>   *Insomnia,*   102
Edna Caster Joll
>   *The Plumcot Tree,*   103
>   *Matthew,*   104
Grace Edgington Jordan
>   *Rest in Peace,*   104
>   *Egg and Ode,*   105
Greg Keeler
>   *American Falls,*   106
Rosemary Klein
>   *Last Words,*   107
Paul LeSage
>   *Hugh's Cafe,*   107
R. J. Petrillo
>   *Weatherwise,*   108
Charles Potts
>   *Alpiner,*   109
Diane Raptosh
>   *Just West of Now,*   110
>   *Idaho,*   111
Vern Rutsala
>   *Gravel, Roads, Fathers, Idaho, Hobos,*
>   *Memory,*   112
>   *The Coast of Idaho,*   113

Words,   *114*
Richard Shelton
 On Lake Pend Oreille,   *115*
 Harry Orchard,   *116*
Ona Siporin
 Boise: The Woman Who Loved Birds,   *118*
 After the Death of the Magician,   *119*
Bill Siverly
 Lewiston,   *119*
Gino Sky
 Gospel Hump,   *120*
John F. Sollers
 An Eye to the Cold,   *120*
 Perpetua,   *121*
 Rosie's Ghost,   *121*
Kim Stafford
 Pocatello Town,   *122*
 Juliaetta Coffee Blues,   *124*
 Villanelle for the Spiders,   *125*
Paul E. Tracy
 Existentialist,   *126*
George Venn
 How to Live Two Days in Osburn, Idaho,   *127*
Lynn Wikle
 A Handmaiden Speaks,   *128*
 The Changeling's Mother,   *129*
Charles David Wright
 The Foolhen,   *130*
 Shaving,   *131*
 There Comes a Wind,   *131*

The Contemporaries   *133*

Introduction,   *133*
Margaret Aho
 Carpal Bones,   *135*
 Pause at Forty,   *135*
Douglas Airmet
 Presence,   *136*
Richard Ardinger
 One Place for Another,   *137*
 Planting Day,   *138*

Report from More's Creek, 139
In Another Country, 139
Diana Armstrong
Spring Spell, 140
Kathleen Armstrong
False Dusk, 140
The Hunter, 141
Lea Baechler
Chase Lake, 142
Taking a Life, 143
Kim Barnes
Women at the Wash Stand, 144
Infestation, 145
Ruth Bull
Boom Town, 146
The Red Dress, 147
Kevin Bushman
Good Morning, 148
Idaho Christmas, 148
Nadine Chapman
On Solitude, 149
Pete Cruz
Indian Poker, 150
Christine Olson Davis
The Little Mud, 150
Zeoma Dvorak
The Story Teller, 151
Bruce Embree
American Hero, 152
April 25, 153
Jack Fleming
Among Old Dancers, 154
*Upon Hearing of the Death of a
Boyhood Friend,* 155
Tina Foriyes
When in Drought, 155
Cabin Note, 156
from Jade Ring, 157
Snowman in Summer, 158
Jane Fritz
I Like Living Alone, 160
Janne Goldbeck
Lava I, 161

Lava II,   161

Winter Song,   162

Carolyn Gravelle

Is the Garden Worth It?,   162

Florence Greathouse

Jackal in Red Stone,   163

Ghost Horses,   164

Gerald Grimmett

Squeeze Play,   165

Chuck Guilford

Maybe the Sky,   165

Dewey Haeder

Love Song in .20 Gauge,   166

Sharon T. Hayes

Success,   167

Left,   167

Skipping Rope in Hayden Lake, Idaho,   168

Borg Hendrickson

Pam,   169

James Hepworth

Silence as a Method of Birth Control,   169

Autumn in Inchelium,   170

Ed Hughes

Settlement,   171

Donnell Hunter

Otto,   172

Louise,   172

A Letter,   173

Randy Huntsberry

Tripwire,   174

Bill Johnson

Moose,   175

Wildrose Cemetery,   175

Robert Johnson

Your Mother's Story,   176

Daryl E. Jones

Un Bel Di,   177

Maidenhair,   178

Joan Juskie-Nellis

Lee Driving through Colorado,   179

Linda Kittell

Island Leaving,   179

Rhonda LaBombard,   180

Alex Kuo
  The River,   *181*
  A Chinaman's Chance,   *182*
Carol Jean Logue
  Cornucopia,   *183*
Stephen Lyons
  Women Out West,   *184*
  House of Wind,   *185*
Linda McAndrew
  Memoirs of an Idaho Falls Carrot
    Snapper,   *186*
Tom McClanahan
  Heartland,   *187*
  The Farm,   *189*
Ron McFarland
  Out Here,   *191*
  Town Marshall,   *192*
  Orgy,   *193*
  A Perfect Day,   *194*
Anne Merkley
  Gold on Blue,   *194*
J. I. Mills
  Ascension,   *195*
Alan Minskoff
  Pounding Nails,   *196*
  Idaho City,   *197*
Rob Moore
  Hometown Bar,   *197*
  Welcome Back,   *198*
Sheryl Noethe
  (untitled),   *199*
Joy Passanante
  Dream-Thief,   *199*
Timothy Pilgrim
  Angle of Repose,   *200*
  Pre-Dawn Vigil at Kootenai Medical Center,   *201*
Scott Preston
  River by Picasso, 1903,   *202*
  Another Story Sun Valley Never Hears,   *203*
Steve Puglisi
  The Arts in Idaho,   *204*
Penelope Reedy
  I Continue,   *204*

Contents

William Studebaker
    Where You Could Live Forever, 205
    Sandpoint, 206
    Jukebox Cave, 207
    Nowhere Near, 208
Ford Swetnam
    One Winter, 209
    Another Winter, 209
    Birthday Metamorphoses, 210
    Pioneer League, Butte vs. Pocatello, 211
Tom Trusky
    Opulence, 211
    Cataplasm, 212
Eberle Umbach
    Theatre in the Heartland, 213
    A Room in Idaho, 214
Lydia Vizcaya
    Where Scuffed Rocks Edge the Road, 215
Norman Weinstein
    Winnemucca, Nevada, 215
    A Place in Place of Father, 216
Fay Wright
    A Window Provides the World, 217
    Christina, 218
Robert Wrigley
    The Sinking of Clay City, 219
    Fireflies, 220
    Heart Attack, 220
    The Drunkard's Path, 221
Harald Wyndham
    Entering the Water, 222
    Swimming in Silence/Drowning in Light, 223
    Graveshift in the Humping Yard, 225
    Seed Store, 226

❦ Preface

IN SELECTING THE OVER TWO HUNDRED FIFTY ENTRIES IN THIS anthology, we have been torn between a desire to be inclusive and what we see as the obligation of all serious editors to be exclusive. We have attempted to offer a full spectrum of the kinds of poetry, both in subject matter or theme and in style or voice, that have been written and are being written by Idaho's poets. As explained in the introductions to the five sections of this book, we have maintained a broad view of what constitutes an "Idaho" poet. Many would argue that Ezra Pound's Idaho birthplace should not entitle him to be included, since he left the state at age a year and a half, never to return, but we have decided that his work should be represented. With a poet like Kenneth O. Hanson, who was born and raised in the state but who has lived most of his adult life elsewhere, the decision to include his work was easy enough, but we determined to place his poem and those of other former residents in the fourth section, leaving the fifth and last section to poets presently living in Idaho.

Because no nation is so mobile as the United States, it should not be surprising that many poets in these pages have been temporary Idaho residents. In fact, Idaho's first poet laureate, Irene Welch Grissom of Idaho Falls, who served between 1923 and 1948, was born in Colorado and retired to California. Many of the poets whose works are included in this volume lived in the state for only a year or two. In those cases we tried to show by our selections that their poetry had been influenced by their residence.

From the outset, however, we agreed that poems selected for this anthology should not be exclusively Idahoan, or even regional in theme or content. Our primary criterion throughout has been the quality of the work. But even though we decided to limit any poet to no more than four poems, we found ourselves making countless difficult decisions. In compiling this anthology we have examined literally thousands of poems, ranging in sources from Native American texts collected by anthropologists and microfilms of early Idaho newspapers to work submitted by contemporary poets in response to news releases and the word-of-mouth network. We think we have discovered much excellent writing but are not so foolish as to suppose that we have found it all. Doubtless some poets never got the word, and we are painfully aware that we have probably made errors in judgment. We have probably said "yes" at times when we should have said "no," and "no" when we should have said "yes."

All anthologies, however, are limited by the visions and tastes of their editors. We have tried to be open-minded and catholic in our selections, including sometimes work that we did not very much "like" personally, but which we recognized as good or effective, given its style, voice, or point of view. Both of us are critics, editors, teachers of poetry, and poets ourselves, so we have approached this work from a variety of angles. Moreover, we have allowed ourselves to disagree with each other and to reflect our varying tastes throughout. We think, too, that our long residence in the two major sections of the state (north and south) has contributed an overall balance to the anthology.

Like all editors, we owe a great debt to those who have gone before us. Bess Foster Smith's *Sunlit Peaks* anthology (Caxton Press, 1931) was especially valuable when it came to the third section, Poets of a New State (1900–1940), and of course James H. Maguire's recent *Literature of Idaho: An Anthology* (Boise State University Press, 1986), which covers all the genres, has been a helpful guide. On a few occasions we found that our selections were the same as Maguire's, but instead of attempting to find other poems that would "do," we have preferred to ratify his editorial tastes in those instances. We have also scanned such anthologies as those compiled by the Idaho Writers League, Harald Wyndham's *Famous Potatoes: Southeast Idaho Poetry* (Blue Scarab Press, 1986), *Idaho+* (Painted Smiles Press, 1987), McFarland's *Eight Idaho Poets* (University of Idaho Press, 1979), and the "Idaho Renaissance" issue of *The Slackwater Review* (Confluence Press, 1983). We have even examined less widely circulated collections such as Clara Corey Caturia's *Potlatch and Other Poems by Poets of Potlatch and Other Places* (Ye Galleon Press, 1979).

In selecting materials for the first section of our anthology we had recourse not only to such recent collections of poems by Native American poets as Joseph Bruchac's *Songs from This Earth on Turtle's Back* (Greenfield Review Press, 1983) and Terry Allen's *Whispering Wind* (Doubleday, 1972), but also to songs, myths, and legends gathered over the past eighty years by such anthropologists and ethnologists as Franz Boas, Edward S. Curtis, Mary Austin, Robert H. Lowie, Deward E. Walker, Jr., and Ella E. Clark.

Our examination of extensive holdings at the Twin Falls Public Library, the University of Idaho Special Collections, the Boise State University Library, and the Idaho State Library in Boise proved time consuming, sometimes exhausting, but definitely rewarding. We are indebted to Gordon Gipson, of Caxton Printers in Caldwell, whose press has published collections of poems by Idaho's poets for over forty years. He has most generously permitted us to reprint work from those books in this collection. And we are especially indebted to many of the poets whose work is included in these pages, not only for their contributions, but also for directing us toward other poets and their work.

Ron McFarland
William Studebaker

❧ *Acknowledgments*

CONTRIBUTORS WERE ENCOURAGED TO SUBMIT BOTH UNPUBLISHED and previously published poems. Most elected to send some of each; consequently, many poems in this anthology have gone through multiple editorial screening. We are indebted to our fellow editors for having prepared the way and to those editors and publishers who have kindly agreed to allow us to reprint the following work from their publications.

Introduction

William Stafford, "Springs Near Hagerman," *Stories That Could Be True* (New York: Harper & Row, 1977).
———, "Coyote," *You and Some Other Characters* (Rexburg: Honeybrook, 1987), 9.
Howard Horowitz, "Idaho," *Close to the Ground* (Eugene, OR: Hulogos'i Communications, 1986), 19.

Native Poems

"Medicine-Song of the Elk" in Edward S. Curtis, ed., *The North American Indians*, Vol. 8 (New York: Johnson Reprint Corp., 1970; rpr. of 1911 text), 60–61.
"The Deluge" in Edward S. Curtis, ed., *The North American Indians*, Vol. 7 (New York: Johnson Reprint Corp., 1970; rpr. of 1911 text), 147–148.
"The Bear Hunter," "The Rock Wren and the Rattlesnake" in Helen Addison Howard, *American Indian Poetry* (Boston: Twayne, 1979), 22, 25.
"Medicine Song," "Death Chant," "Wyakin Song from a Male Buffalo" in Melda Ann Williams, "Historical Background and Musical Analysis of Thirty Selected Nez Perce Songs," unpublished University of Idaho Master of Music thesis, 1967. Pages 84, 185, 61.
"Three Songs of Mad Coyote" in Jerome Rothenberg, ed., *Shaking the Pumpkin* (Garden City, NY: Doubleday, 1972), 275.
"Smohalla Speaks" in Margot Astrov, ed., *American Indian Prose and Poetry* (New York: Capricorn, 1962), 85.
"Coyote and the Swallowing Monster" in Franz Boas, *Folk-Tales of the Salishan and Sahaptin Tribes; Memoirs of the American Folk-Lore Society* (1917), 148–149.
"Origin of the Sweat House," "The Craters of the Moon," "Lake Coeur

d'Alene," "The Little People" in Ella E. Clark, *Indian Legends from the Northern Rockies* (Norman: University of Oklahoma Press, 1966), 49–50, 209–210, 124, 129–130.

Phil George, "Old Man, The Sweat Lodge" in Terry Allen, ed., *The Whispering Wind* (Garden City, NY: Doubleday, 1972), 115.

———— "Name Giveaway," "Morning Beads," "Call of the Flute," *Kautsas* (Spalding: P.N.N.P.F.A., 1978), np.

"Neither Spirit Nor Bird," "Glyphs," "Lament of a Man for his Son," "The Grass on the Mountain" in Mary Austin, *The American Rhythm* (Boston: Houghton, Mifflin, 1930), 109, 107–108, 102, 88.

"Rain Song," "Aspen Song" in Eleanor B. Heady, *Sage Smoke: Tales of the Shoshoni-Bannock Indians* (Chicago: Follett, 1973), 86, 87.

"Coyote and the Rock" in Deward E. Walker, Jr., *Myths of the Idaho Indians* (Moscow: University of Idaho Press, 1982), 153–154.

Janet Campbell Hale, "Backyard Swing," "Desmet, Idaho, March 1969" in Joseph Bruchac, ed., *Songs from This Earth on Turtle's Back* (Greenfield Center, NY: Greenfield Review 1983), 85, 88.

Pioneer Poets

Poems with sources in early Idaho newspapers are identified in the text.

Clarence E. Eddy, "Springtime in Idaho," *The Pinnacle of Parnassus* (Salt Lake City: Tribune Printing, 1902), 24–25.

H. F. Johnson, "The Israelite's Last Mule Ride" in John Carrey, ed., *Salmon River Prose and Poetry* (Grangeville, ID: Idaho City Free Press, 1970).

———— "Farewell to Idaho," *Poems of Idaho* (Weiser: Signal Job Printing House, 1895), 14–17.

Poets of a New State

Vardis Fisher, "Dick Rowe," "Hank Radder" in Bess Foster Smith, ed., *Sunlit Peaks* (Caldwell, ID: Caxton, 1931), 74, 75.

———— "Joe Hunter" in Dorys C. Grover, *Vardis Fisher: The Novelist as Poet* (New York: Revisionist Press, 1973), 49– 50.

Donald Burnie, "Eva Kelly," "Harry Gale," "Wild Moll" *Tsceminicum: Snake River People* (Missoula, MT: Harold G. Merriam, 1930), 27, 31, 44.

Ezra Pound, "Moeurs Contemporaines," *Personae* (New York: New Directions, 1971), 178–182.

Irene Welch Grissom, "Clearing Sagebrush," *Verse of the New West* (Caldwell: Caxton, 1931), 3.

Janet Ellen Miller, "The Big Boss"; Paul Croy, "River Pig"; Ruth Bernice Mead, "Mountain Interlude"; Keith Barrette, "Rural Etching" in Bess Foster Smith, ed., *Sunlit Peaks: An Anthology of Idaho Verse* (Caldwell: Caxton, 1931), 130, 146–147, 141, 39.

Yvor Winters, "Nocturne," "The Journey," *Collected Poems* (Denver: Alan Swallow, 1960), 28, 66–67.

Carol Ryrie Brink, "The Fairy Wife," *Poetry*, 28 (September 1926), 312–313.

———, "Foggy Day at the Beach," "Thoughts on Eating an Apple," *Shreds and Patches*.

Jean Chalmers Donaldson, "Young Farm Wife," "Back Street Autumn," "Hollyhocks," *Cup of Stars* (Atlanta: Banner, 1939), 12, 13, 46.

———, "Velvet Foil," *Bridge Against Time* (Dallas: Avalon, 1945), 36.

Forrest Anderson, "springboard as a waterfront cafe," "definitions," "vol fantasque," *Sea Pieces and Other Poems* (New York: Cassowary, 1935), 3, 38, 39.

Bess Foster Smith, "Country Store," *The Checkered Tablecloth* (Caldwell: Caxton, 1937), 48.

Norman Macleod, "Evening above the Snake," "Ring around the Syringas," *Selected Poems* (Boise: Ahsahta, 1975), 14, 11–12.

Edna Gillespie, "Wall-Flower," *The North American Book of Verse* Vol. 4 (New York: Henry Harrison, 1939), 64.

E. A. Brubacher, "Joe Weaver of Owyhee" in Bess Foster Smith, ed., *Songs of the Saddle and Trails into Lonesome Land* (Caldwell: Caxton, nd), 53.

Amy Woodward Fisher, "Rain in Harvest," *Two Stars in a Window* (Caldwell: Caxton, 1946), 45.

Edith M. Roberts, "Idaho Potato Field," *The North American Book of Verse*, Vol. 4 (New York: Henry Harrison, 1939), 69.

The Third Generation

Duane Ackerson, "Beforehand," "Weathering," *Weathering* (Reno: West Coast Poetry Review, 1973), 9, 7.

James Ater, "mountain vigil," *9 Poems* (self-published, nd), np.

James Brock, "The Growth of Mathematics," *College English;* "The Recognition of Beasts," *The Louisville Reader*.

Ed Dorn, "Home on the Range, February, 1962," "Chronicle," *Collected Poems, 1956–1974* (San Francisco: Four Seasons, 1983), 43–44, 133–134.

Carolyn S. Foote, "Widow," "Reflections," *Selected Poems* (Boise: cold-drill books, 1984), 13, 15.

Sudie Stuart Hager, "A Spider Web in a Rose Garden," *Earthbound* (Dallas: Kaleidograph, 1947), 40.

Kenneth O. Hanson, "Montana," *The Distance Anywhere* (Seattle: University of Washington Press, 1967), 82.

Jim Heynen, "Traveling through Idaho on Opening Day," *A Suitable Church* (Port Townsend, WA: Copper Canyon, 1981), 79.

Bonnie Cochrane Hirsch, "Me an Mason Williams, Down the Garden Path" in Ronald E. McFarland, ed., *Eight Idaho Poets* (Moscow: University of Idaho Press, 1979), 38.

———, "Knighthood in Grangeville," *Runes for Another Year* (Boise: self-published chapbook, 1986).

Jim Irons, "Insomnia," *cold-drill.*

Edna Caster Joll, "The Plumcot Tree," "Matthew," *The Plumcot Tree* (Caldwell: Caxton, 1965), 27, 113.

Grace Edgington Jordan, "Rest in Peace," "Egg and Ode," *Idaho Reflections* (Boise: Boise State University, 1984), 22–23, 27.

Greg Keeler, "American Falls," *American Falls* (Lewiston: Confluence, 1988), 55; *Prairie Schooner* (Winter 1979/80).

Paul LeSage, "Hugh's Cafe," *Outpost*, 1 (Spring 1974).

Charles Potts, "Alpiner," *Rocky Mountain Man* (New York: The Smith, 1978), 9–10.

Diane Raptosh, "Just West of Now," *Michigan Quarterly Review* (Winter 1987).

———, "Idaho," *Mid-American Review.*

Vern Rutsala, "Gravel, Roads, Fathers, Idaho, Hobos, Memory," "The Coast of Idaho," "Words," *Walking Home from the Icehouse* (Pittsburgh: Carnegie-Mellon University, 1981), 47–48, 51–52, 31–32.

Richard Shelton, "On Lake Pend Oreille," *The New Yorker* August 23, 1969.

———, "Harry Orchard," *Selected Poems, 1969–1981* (Pittsburgh: University of Pittsburgh Press, 1982), 172–174.

Ona Siporin, "Boise: The Woman Who Loved Birds," *Cloudline: landscript visions of the far western eye* (1986–87).

Gino Sky, "Gospel Hump," poem card (Boise: Limberlost, 1987).

Kim Stafford, "Juliaetta Coffee Blues," *Places and Stories* (Pittsburgh: Carnegie-Mellon, 1987), 20–21.

———, "Villanelle for the Spiders," *A Gypsy's History of the World* (Port Townsend, WA: Copper Canyon, 1976) np.

Paul Tracy, "Existentialist," *Owyhee Horizons* (Caldwell: Caxton, 1968), 14.

George Venn, "How to Live Two Days in Osburn, Idaho," *Off the Main Road* (Portland: Prescott Street, 1978).

Charles David Wright, "The Foolhen," "There Comes a Wind," in Ronald E. McFarland, ed., *Eight Idaho Poets* (Moscow: University of Idaho Press, 1979), 24, 18–19.

———, "Shaving," *Clearing Away* (Lewiston: Confluence, 1980), 32; *Spoon River Quarterly.*

The Contemporaries

Margaret Aho, "Carpal Bones," "Pause at Forty," *Northwest Review*, Vol. 24, #1 (1986).

Richard Ardinger, "One Place for Another," "Planting Day," *One Place for Another* (Lewiston: Confluence Press, 1983), np.

———, "Report from More's Creek," *Report from More's Creek* (Story, WY: Dooryard, 1986), np.

———, "Another Country," poem card series (Boise: Limberlost, 1987).

Kim Barnes, "Women at the Wash Stand," *Seattle Review* (Spring 1984).

———, "Infestation," *Snapdragon*, 8 (Fall 1984), 3.

Ruth Bull, "Boom Town," *Snapdragon*, 7 (Fall 1983), 4–5.

Nadine Chapman, "On Solitude," *Plainswoman* (January 1987), 16.

Christine Olson Davis, "The Little Mud," forthcoming in *cold - drill*.

Bruce Embree, "American Hero," Harald Wyndham, ed., *Famous Potatoes: Southeast Idaho Poetry* (Pocatello: Blue Scarab, 1986), np.

Jack Fleming, "Among Old Dancers," *Webster Review* (Spring 1987).

———, "Upon Hearing of the Death of a Boyhood Friend," *Louisville Review* (Spring 1987).

Tina Foriyes, "Snowman in Summer," *Eight Idaho Poets* (Moscow: University of Idaho Press, 1979), 128–130.

Carolyn Gravelle, "Is the Garden Worth It?," *Snapdragon*, 3 (Spring 1980), 12–13.

Florence Greathouse, "Jackal in Red Stone," *Black Fly Review*, 6 (1985), 32.

———, "Ghost Horses," *Plainsong*, 6 (Spring 1985), 41.

Sharon T. Hayes, "Success," *Writer's Chapbook*, 4 (January 1986), 28.

James R. Hepworth, "Silence as a Method of Birth Control," "Autumn in Inchelium," *Silence as a Method of Birth Control* (Lewiston: Confluence Press, 1977), np.

Donnell Hunter, "Otto," "Louise," "A Letter," *The Frog in Our Basement* (Rexburg: Honeybrook, 1984), 2, 5, 1.

Randy Huntsberry, "Tripwire," *Ascent*, 13, #1 (1987).

Bill Johnson, "Moose," *Quarterly West*, 22 (Spring/Summer 1986).

Robert Johnson, "Your Mother's Story," forthcoming in *Hubbub*.

Daryl E. Jones, "Maidenhair," *New Orleans Review*, 12 (1986). By Loyola University, New Orleans.

Linda Kittell, "Rhonda LaBombard," *Snapdragon*, 7 (Fall 1983), 26.

Alex Kuo, "A Chinaman's Chance," *Changing the River* (Berkeley, CA: 1986), 92–93.

Linda McAndrews, "Memoirs of an Idaho Falls Carrot Snapper," *Idaho+: Contemporary Poetry from the American West* (Boise: Painted Smiles, 1987), 25.

Tom McClanahan, "Heartland," "The Farm," *From the Green Horseshoe* (Columbia, SC: University of South Carolina Press, 1988).

Ron McFarland, "Out Here," forthcoming in *Christian Science Monitor*.

———, "Town Marshall," *Idaho English Journal*, 8 (Spring 1985), 24.

———, "A Perfect Day," *Ascent*, 12 (1987), 39.

Anne Merkley, "Gold on Blue," *Rendezvous*, 4 (Winter 1969).

J. I. Mills, "Ascension," *Kayak*, 64 (1984).

Timothy Pilgrim, "Pre-Dawn Vigil at Kootenai Medical Center," *Trestle Creek Review*.

Scott Preston, "River by Picasso, 1903," *Snapdragon*, 7 (Spring 1984), 12.

Steve Puglisi, "The Arts in Idaho," Harald Wyndham, ed., *Famous Potatoes: Southeast Idaho Poetry* (Pocatello: Blue Scarab, 1986), np.

William Studebaker, "Where You Could Live Forever," *Times-News* (December 20, 1984), 36.

Acknowledgments

————, "Sandpoint," *Tar River Poetry*, 24 (1984).

————, "Jukebox Cave," *Slackwater Review* (Spring 1984), 101.

Ford Swetnam, "One Winter," "Another Winter," Harald Wyndham, ed., *Famous Potatoes: Southeast Idaho Poetry* (Pocatello: Blue Scarab, 1986), np.

Norman Weinstein, "Winnemucca, Nevada," *Nigredo* (Barrytown, NY: 1982), 54. Copyright 1982 by Norman Weinstein.

Fay Wright, "Christina," *Out of Season* (Lewiston: Confluence, 1981), np.

Robert Wrigley, "The Sinking of Clay City," *The Sinking of Clay City* (Port Townsend, WA: Copper Canyon, 1979), 50.

————, "Fireflies," "Heart Attack," *Moon in a Mason Jar* (Urbana: University of Illinois Press, 1986), 27, 9–10.

Harald Wyndham, "Entering the Water," *Pebble Creek* (Lewiston: Confluence Press, 1978), np.

————, "Swimming in Silence/Drowning in Light," *Famous Potatoes: Southeast Idaho Poetry* (Pocatello: Blue Scarab, 1986), np.

————, "Seed Store," *Ohio Gothic* (Pocatello: Blue Scarab, 1985), np.

❦ Introduction

Time-Lapse Poetry

LITERATURE, THAT HANDLE ON LIFE AS IT FEELS IN THE LIVING OF it, has a flickering appearance in the West. In Idaho, speeded-up history has ratcheted poetry forward in jumps, as reflected by the divisions in the present collection.

The first phase is the most striking and most enigmatic for all of us today: how can we enter that cavern of realization that Native Americans, "the people," felt when they used sound to interact with mystery? We can't hear the music; we can't learn how to allow ourselves their talent for immersion-in-the-world. Fragments put onto a page to encompass that richness in this first section are reminders only, reminders of a way to live that now escapes us. Can we ever lean forward to animals and places and let language float everything together again?

Maybe true poetry permeated all living back in those days, and we have been trying to get back there ever since. And now later writers who follow Native American themes or materials, no matter how hard they try, can't help bringing to their work a changed consciousness that has separated our poetry from other parts of our lives.

Such a separation marks the early fragments of literature written by pioneers. Although we cannot help feeling that people in any time or place do have their visions and their lucky passages of language, and though the pioneers brought along with them souvenirs and snatches of literature, their imitations of such treasures bear only the trappings of the past. Audiences on the frontier reach so eagerly for nostalgia that they miss the connections with today that give life to the doing of art.

That power to link present experience to opportunities in language did not appear decisively, to my way of reading, until Vardis Fisher, whose work appears here in section three, Poets of a New State. At this point, working in a standard form but straining it for his purpose, an Idaho writer nails down Idaho statement in a sonnet on Joe Hunter: ". . . his gnarled and calloused hands had wrought / A deep and quiet holiness of work."

From 1940 on Idaho writers have flourished and made their individual ways into the life of their times as enhanced by the power of the language we speak. Like those earliest people who possessed both immediacy and tradition, current poets are bringing those elements together in the dailiness of their writing. No corner of the state lacks for voices that speak directly to an audience grown confident and receptive.

As a sporadic Idahoan myself I feel the vigor of place and encounter combined, and want to get into the chorus:

Springs Near Hagerman

Water leaps from lava near Hagerman,
piles down riverward over rock
reverberating tons of exploded shock
    out of that stilled world.

We halted there once. In that cool
we drank, for back and where we had to go
lay our jobs and Idaho,
    lying far from such water.

At work when I vision that sacred land—
the vacation of mist over its rock wall—
I go blind with hope. That plumed fall
    is bright to remember.

And:

Coyote

My left hind-
foot
    steps
in the track of my right
fore-
    foot
and my hind-right
foot
    steps
in the track of my
fore-left
      foot
and so on, for miles—

Me paying no attention, while
my nose   rides along letting
the full report, the
whole blast of the countryside
come along toward me
on rollers of scent,   and—

I come home with a chicken or
a rabbit and sit up
singing all night with my friends.
It's baroque, my life, and
I tell it on the mountain.

I wouldn't trade it for yours.

William Stafford

The following poem is by Howard Horowitz, a biogeographer holding a Ph.D. from the University of Oregon, who traveled Idaho's
forests as a contract reforestation worker for the U.S. Forest Service
between 1973 and 1982:

Idaho

It's Great
to plant
trees in
Idaho, when
snow melt roars
in the Clearwater,
& when frost crisps
the brushfields red
in the Bitterroots.
Steep ridges of shrub
and rock, young larch
and fir, bleached snags:
remember the great fire
of 1910, when Pulaski
   forced his men into a
    mineshaft, to survive;
  when the train got away
from Wallace on flaming tracks.
Luck still touches some of us: remember
   the crummy, upside-down in a pond (the consequence of driving to camp without headlights
after the bar closed in Elk City). Good money
and good times on a Kelly Creek clearcut, in a
Pierce tavern, in the Grangeville Hotel. Remember
swimming holes on the Salmon, hot springs baths,
the log truck driver dancing with his daughter,
a bear with rose hip scat, a meteor shower in
Orion, the woman that night in Orofino. Remember
Idaho is too Great to pass nonstop on the freeway.

❦ Native Poems

Introduction

FROM AT LEAST ONE PERSPECTIVE IDAHO'S INDIANS, NATIVE AMER-
icans, or, as they refer to themselves, "the people," have no true
poetry. Theirs is an oral tradition, and their cultures are communal in
nature. The image of the solitary poet, often a bit on the eccentric
side, pouring his or her individual genius onto the page for a reading
audience is antithetical to the image we should devise for the Nez
Perce or the Shoshone-Bannock. It would be easy simply to dis-
regard any Native American Poetry except that written in English by
contemporary poets with some tribal affiliation.

But from another perspective nearly all the legends and myths of
Idaho's earliest residents are poetry. Their simple songs, often no
more than two lines repeated over and over, are close to the pure
lyric tradition that underlies Western poetry. Their myths and legends, retold and taught for both entertainment and instruction, are
close to the narrative poem. Few of their legends strike the reader as
mere "stories," being too elliptical and too much a part of sheer
imagination to fit comfortably into that niche. Reminiscent of folk
tales and fairy stories at times, they are closest perhaps to the world
we encounter in Ovid's *Metamorphoses*.

We have decided, therefore, to represent the major tribes that
inhabited Idaho before the coming of the White man by a selection of
songs and of legends or myths taken from various sources, usually
from anthropologists who followed the lead of Franz Boas in taking
down the words of tribal "informants." These "poems" are, of course,
translations, sometimes by an anthropologist or linguist and sometimes by the Native teller. Obviously there is no way to do justice to
this sort of material, but we are pleased to follow those who have
labored to remind us that culture in the Northwest did not begin with
the fur trappers, the travels of Lewis and Clark, or the gold rush. To
these poems we are adding some work by contemporary poets from
the state who have tribal affiliation, our point being that their poetry,
their voice, lives.

What images should we try to conjure when reading the translated
words of Idaho's first poets? We might think of a father or mother, or
more likely a grandparent, telling stories to children around a camp-

fire, particularly in winter, the time of storytelling for most of the tribes. Or we might imagine a boy on his vision quest, listening for the song of his spirit animal (that is, his "wyakin"), and we could imagine that same boy as a young man hunting or raiding an enemy camp, singing that song (perhaps not aloud) to raise his spirits or rouse his courage. We should also consider the mother crooning a soft, simple lullaby to her restless baby. And we might conjure up a medicine man singing his song of healing. At last, or perhaps preeminently, we should think of the assembled tribe chanting and singing for rain or for success in hunting or fishing or in battle. The "signature" given such poems here will always be tribal, including "Nez Perce," "Shoshone," "Paiute," "Bannock," "Kutenai," "Coeur d'Alene," or "The People."

For the contemporary Native American poet that signature is more complex. Like the protagonists of James Welch's or Leslie Silko's novels, he or she is caught between cultures, as is obvious in Janet Hale's memory of her father's wake held in Desmet. Matthew Arnold wrote in the 1850s of himself as a man "Wandering between two worlds, one dead, / The other powerless to be born." The poems of Nez Perce poet Phil George suggest that his world is not dead. As he concludes in "Prelude to Memorial Song," dedicated to the descendants of the Nez Perce War of 1877, "I am alive. / Nemipu are breathing humans: / We Are Alive."

Native Poems

Nez Perce

What complicates the use of Native song in a collection of poems in the Western or European tradition may be illustrated by the following example from Edward S. Curtis's *The North American Indian*, Vol. 8, which appeared in 1911. We offer the "Medicine-Song of the Elk" in three versions: as transcribed from the Nez Perce, as translated literally, and as adapted by Curtis in an effort to transfer the meaning of the song as a Nez Perce might understand it. But even these three versions are not sufficient to account for the song, as the musical score might also appropriately be added (it is available in Curtis's book). To a much greater extent than is the case in most Western poems, what is implicit is far more significant than what is explicit in the words. In many of the poems that follow, readers may be reminded of the extreme understatement and elusiveness of oriental poetry.

Medicine-Song of the Elk

Awiyihiyi! Hilayihiyi wihina. Awiyihiyi! Hilayihiyi wihina.
Pasotainaks! Hilayihiyi wihina.
Awiyihiyi! Hilayihiyi wihina. Awiyihiyi! Hilayihiyi wihina.
Awiyihiyi! Hilayihiyi wihina.
Pitiwatainaks! Hilayihiyi wihina.

Elk! Eagle moving. Elk! Eagle moving.
Feet planted deep in the ground! Eagle moving.
Elk! Eagle moving. Elk! Eagle moving.
Elk! Eagle moving.
Tips of horns touching the ground! Eagle moving.

"Eagle, and all the other predatory creatures of the
Waptipas, have forced Elk into a corner. There he turns
and makes this song. Right above him is Eagle, with wings
outspread, while the Wolves and the other animals are
pressing about Elk, trying to kill him. His legs are spread,
his feet deep in the ground, and his head is lowered so
that his horns touch the earth. He will not die without

hurting somebody. Eagle holds himself motionless in the air, watching and waiting for a chance to swoop down and take the best part of the prey for himself. Elk stands with bloody legs, torn by the Wolves. His back is against the cliff."

The Bear Hunter

This bear was my friend
Living in the great woods,
I did not kill him,
Too-na-a-ta-hoe.
He committed self-death
By coming before the arrow.
Gus-nee-whey, oh-ta-hee-na-ho-hus-hee-
Perhaps hunger that was in my camp
He knew, and came that our lives
Might be strengthened.
I did not kill this bear,
My friend of the woods,
I did not kill this bear,
My friend of the woods.

The Rock Wren and the Rattlesnake

You have a blunt nose,
Your head is flat and ugly,
You crawl in among the rocks,
Your home is in the dark ground,
Your color is dull and faded,
Wan-a-hey—wan-a-yay.

You are bad all the time,
Nobody likes you,
Your breath is poisonous,
Your bite is deadly,
You hide like a coward.

Come out from your hiding,
I am not afraid of you!
Wan-a-hey, wan-a-hey,
Wan-a-yay, wan-a-yay,
Wan-a-yay!

Medicine Song

A little winter bird
floating down the river on a piece of ice
says, "I am testing this ice raft.
I'm above winter
and I'm more powerful than winter."
This bird has power to take sickness out.
It is looking for the sickness
and challenges it.
The bird is strong.
It will get the mark.

Death Chant

Now his spirit is traveling.
Going over the mountains.
He travels through the evening
Riding the yellow clouds.

Wyakin Song from a Male Buffalo

Through my life I mourn.
Buffalo challenges this life
whether it's tough or good.
When the daylight starts to come
at break of day,
it lays a shadow over me
that reflects my life.
My soul sings.
The days are going by,
but I can challenge any hurt
because my song
takes care of all my needs.
I can stand all the hardships.

Three Songs of Mad Coyote (WYAKIN)

1.
Ravening Coyote comes,
red hands, red mouth,
necklace of eye-balls!
2.
Mad Coyote
madly sings,
then the west wind roars!
3.
Daybreak finds me,
eastern daybreak finds me
the meaning of that song:
with blood-stained mouth
comes mad Coyote!

Chief Joseph's surrender speech, delivered in 1877 at the end of the
Nez Perce War, is so familiar ("I will fight no more forever") that we
have decided not to reprint it here, though it has an established place
in the canon of the Nez Perce literary heritage. We offer instead a
speech by the charismatic medicine man, Smohalla, who was active
in the mid-nineteenth century and who bitterly opposed acceptance
of White ways.

Smohalla Speaks

My young men shall never work. Men who work cannot
dream, and wisdom comes in dreams.

You ask me to plow the ground. Shall I take a knife and
tear my mother's breast? Then when I die she will not
take me to her bosom to rest.

You ask me to dig for stone. Shall I dig under her skin
for bones? Then when I die I cannot enter her body to be
born again.

You ask me to cut grass and make hay and sell it, and
be rich like white men. But how dare I cut off my
mother's hair?

It is a bad law, and my people cannot obey it. I want
my people to stay with me here. All the dead men will
come to life again. We must wait here in the house of our
fathers and be ready to meet them in the body of our
mother.

One problem inherent in the transcription of Native myths and legends is that their "literary" (that is, their rhetorical and figurative or metaphorical) character will vary with the teller or informant. In effect, some people's accounts of events are more "colorful" than those of others. Moreover, we have no way of accounting for what is added or subtracted by the person, usually an anthropologist, recording the narrations. The version of the creation of the Nez Perce people given below is one of the best known of their legends, and it exists in many variants. This one is from Franz Boas's *Folk-Tales of the Salishan and Sahaptin Tribes* (1917).

Coyote and the Swallowing Monster

Coyote came back westward through Idaho. On his way he heard that a monster was swallowing the people. Coyote tied himself with a wild grape-vine in three different places, and then crawled over the mountains to see the monster. He hid behind a bundle of grass that he carried in front of himself. He had pitch and fire-sticks in his quiver. He met the monster at Kamiah. Then he mocked him, saying, "Iltswetsix [that was the monster's name], let us swallow each other!" The monster was so surprised that he did not know what to say. He told Coyote to swallow him first. Coyote, however, said that he prefered him to begin, but finally he gave in and agreed to swallow the monster first. Coyote drew in his breath, and the monster could hardly withstand the suction. He said, "Doggone you! you are stronger than I thought." Coyote then said, "now it is your turn." The monster tried hard to move Coyote, but he was tied fast. Coyote then tried a second time, and was able to move the monster a little. When the monster tried again, one of the ropes that held Coyote broke. The next time all the ropes broke, and Coyote was drawn towards the monster. He argued with him, because they could not agree on the way Coyote should enter his body. The monster tried to get him to go in through the anus or the ears; Coyote, however, insisted on going through the mouth, and at last the monster consented. He opened his mouth, and Coyote went in. Inside he met Rattlesnake, who wanted to bite him. Coyote trampled him under foot, thereby flattening his nose, and reviled him for not biting the monster. Farther he met Grizzly-Bear, and reproached him for not killing the monster. Finally he reached the place where the monster's heart was hanging. He stabbed it with his knife. The monster now tried to coax Coyote to come out. He refused, however, and proceeded to build a fire directly under the heart. Then he cut it. He ordered the people to get ready to step out before the monster should die. They went out, Coyote last of all. The monster may be seen in Kamiah to-day, and the heart is there too.

Then Coyote decided to cut up the monster and to divide it among the people. Out of its feet he made the Blackfeet. The Crow, the Sioux, and the Bannock were all made out of different parts of its body. While Coyote was standing there, some one said, "What did you take yourself?" and he replied, "To be wise (?)." Then he called for water. He washed his hands and scattered the water, saying, "You shall be the Nez Perces, a small tribe, but you shall be the most powerful of all the people."

The following legend or myth on the origin of the sacred sweat house is a Nez Perce account recorded in 1896 by Lewis Williams and reprinted in Ella E. Clark's *Indian Legends from the Northern Rockies* (1966).

Origin of the Sweat House

Long ago, in the days of the animal people, Sweat House was a man. He foresaw the coming of the human beings, the real inhabitants of the earth. So one day he called all the animal people together, to give each one a name and to tell him his duties.

In the council, Sweat House stood up and made his speech: "We have lived on this earth for a long while, but we shall not be in our present condition much longer. A different people are coming to live here. We must part from each other and go to different places. Each of you must decide whether you wish to belong to the animal beings that walk or that fly, that creep or that swim. You may now make your choice."

Then Sweat House turned to Elk. "You will first come this way, Elk. What do you wish to be?"

"I wish to be just what I am—an elk."

"Let us see you run or gallop," said Sweat House.

So Elk galloped off in a graceful manner, and then returned.

"You are all right," decided Sweat House. "You are an elk."

Elk galloped off, and the rest saw no more of him.

Sweat House called Eagle to him and asked, "What do you wish to be, Eagle?"

"I wish to be just what I am—an eagle."

"Let us see you fly," replied Sweat House.

Eagle flew, rising higher and higher, with hardly a ripple on his outstretched wings.

Sweat House called him back and said to him, "You are an eagle. You will be king over all the birds of the air. You will soar in the sky. You will live on the crags and peaks of the highest mountains. The human beings will admire you."

Happy with that decision, Eagle flew away. Everybody watched him until he disappeared in the sky.

"I wish to be like Eagle," Bluejay told Sweat House.

Wanting to give everyone a chance, Sweat House said again, "Let us see you fly."

Bluejay flew into the air, trying to imitate the easy, graceful flight of Eagle. But he failed to keep himself balanced and was soon flapping his wings.

Noticing his awkwardness, Sweat House called Bluejay back to him and said, "A jay is a jay. You will have to be contented as you are."

When Bear came forward, Sweat House said to him, "You will be known among human beings as a very fierce animal. You will kill and eat people, and they will fear you."

Bear then went off into the woods and has since been known as a fierce animal.

Then to all the walking creatures except Coyote, and all the flying creatures, to all the animals and birds, all the snakes and frogs and turtles and fish, Sweat House gave names, and the creatures scattered.

After they had gone, Sweat House called Coyote to him and said, "You have been wise and cunning. A man to be feared you have been. This earth shall become like the air, empty and void, yet your name shall last forever. The new human beings who are to come will hear your name and will say, 'Yes, Coyote was great in his time.' Now what do you wish to be?"

"I have lived long enough as Coyote," he replied. "I want to be noble like Eagle or Elk or Cougar."

Sweat House let him show what he could do. First
Coyote tried his best to fly like Eagle, but he could only
jump around, this way and that way. He could not fly, the
poor fellow. Then he tried to imitate the Elk in his
graceful gallop. For a short distance he succeeded, but
soon he returned to his own gait. He ran a little way,
stopped short, and looked around.

"You look exactly like yourself, Coyote," laughed Sweat
House. "You will be a coyote."

Poor Coyote ran off, howling, to some unknown place.
Before he got out of sight, he stopped, turned his head,
and stood—just like a coyote.

Sweat House, left alone, spoke to himself: "All now are
gone, and the new people will be coming soon. When
they arrive, they should find something that will give them
strength and power."

"I will place myself on the ground, for the use of the
human beings who are to come. Whoever will visit me
now and then, to him I will give power. He will become
great in war and great in peace. He will have success in
fishing and in hunting. To all who come to me for
protection I will give strength and power."

Sweat House spoke with earnestness. Then he lay down,
on his hands and knees, and waited for the first people.
He has lain that way ever since and has given power to all
who have sought it from him.

Phil George, author of the following four poems, is a Nez Perce poet
who was born and raised in Lapwai and presently lives in Coulee
Dam, Washington. Some of his poems accompany exhibits in the Nez
Perce museum at Spalding.

PHIL GEORGE

Old Man, The Sweat Lodge

"This small lodge is now alive,
The womb of our mother, Earth.
The blackness in which we sit,
The ignorance of our impure minds,
These burning stones are
The coming of a new life."
Near my heart I place his words.

Naked, like an infant at birth, I crouch,
Cuddled upon fresh straw and boughs.
Confessing, I recall all evil deeds.
For each sin I sprinkle water on fire-hot stones;
Their hissing is a special song and I know
The place from which Earth's seeds grow is alive.

Old man, the Sweat Lodge heals the sick;
Brings good fortune to one deserving.
Sacred steam rises—vapor fills my very being—
My pores slime out their dross.
After chanting prayers to the Great Spirit,
I lift a blanket to the East;
Through this door dawns wisdom.

Cleansed, I dive into icy waters.
Pure, I rinse away unworthy yesterday.
"My son, walk straight in this new life.
Youth I help to retain in you.
Return soon. Visit an old one.
Now, think clean, feel clean, be happy."
I thank you, Old Man, the Sweat Lodge.

Name Giveaway

That teacher gave me a new name . . . again.
    She never even had feasts or a giveaway!

Still I do not know what "George" means;
    and now she calls me: "Phillip."

    TWO FLOCKS OF GEESE LIGHTING UPON
    STILL WATERS
    must be a name too hard to remember.

Morning Beads

Into drops of crystal dew
Displayed upon a lily leaf,
I see tonight's desire.

One bead . . . another . . .
Trickles down, down,
Embellishing the camas stem.

With the jeweler of the dawn
Mother strings beads in sunrise hues
On moccasins I will wear tonight.

Call of the Flute

When blue twilight smoke is straight
As tepee poles, listen for melody.

Smooth as this flowing stream,
I will play my flute for you.

Gentle my fingers move on the flute.
So we will touch when we meet.

Come, to the signal of killdeer crying,
Diving, trying to chase me away.

Harmless, we will love near their nest,
Embraced in a nest all our own.

My open buffalo robe awaits;
This mellow tune I play for you.

Shoshone-Bannock and Northern Paiute

The Bannocks, a tribe of Northern Paiutes, have been closely associated with the Shoshone, who speak a different language, since their settlement on the Fort Hall reservation in the 19th century. The first four poems or songs in this collection are "reexpressions" composed by Mary Austin and published in *The American Rhythm* (1923). Her work might more properly be considered "adaptations" of the oral songs than literal translations.

Neither Spirit Nor Bird (SHOSHONE)

Neither spirit nor bird:
That was my flute you heard
Last night by the river.
When you came with your wicker jar
Where the river drags the willows,
That was my flute you heard,
Wacoba, Wacoba,
Calling, Come to the willows!

Neither the wind nor a bird
Rustled the lupine blooms.
That was my blood you heard
Answer your garment's hem
Whispering through the grasses;
That was my blood you heard
By the wild rose under the willows.

That was no beast that stirred,
That was my heart you heard,
Pacing to and fro
In the ambush of my desire,
To the music my flute let fall.
Wacoba, Wacoba,
That was my heart you heard
Leaping under the willows.

Glyphs (PAIUTE)

I
A girl wearing a green ribbon,—
As if it had been my girl.
—The green ribbon I gave her for remembrance—
Knowing all the time it was not my girl,
Such was the magic of that ribbon,
Suddenly,
My girl existed inside me!

II
Your face is strange,
And the smell of your garments,

17

But your soul is familiar;
As if in dreams our thoughts
Had visited one another.

Often from unremembering sleep
I wake delicately glowing.
Now I know what my heart has been doing.

Now I know why when we met
It slipped
So easily into loving.

III
Truly buzzards
Around my sky are circling!

For my soul festers,
And an odor of corruption
Betrays me to disaster.

Meanness, betrayal and spite
Come flockwise,
To make me aware
Of sickness and death within me.
My sky is full of the dreadful sound
Of the wings of unsuccesses.

Lament of a Man for His Son (PAIUTE)

Son, my son!

I will go up to the mountain
And there I will light a fire
To the feet of my son's spirit,
And there I will lament him;
Saying,
O my son,
What is my life to me, now you are departed!

Son, my son,
In the deep earth
We softly laid thee in a Chief's robe,
In a warrior's gear.

Surely there,
In the spirit land
Thy deeds attend thee!
Surely,
The corn comes to the ear again!

But I, here,
I am the stalk that the seed-gatherers
Descrying empty, afar, left standing.
Son, my son!
What is life to me, now you are departed?

The Grass on the Mountain (PAIUTE)

Oh, long, long
The snow has possessed the mountains.

The deer have come down and the big-horn,
They have followed the Sun to the south
To feed on the mesquite pods and the bunch grass.
Loud are the thunder drums
In the tents of the mountains.

Oh, long, long
Have we eaten the *chia* seeds
And dried deer's flesh of the summer killing.
We are wearied of our huts
And the smoky smell of our garments.

We are sick with desire of the sun
And the grass of the mountain.

Rain Song

Breath of the mountains,
Blow down the valleys,
Blow rain to the lowlands
And grass to the prairies.

Aspen Song

Breeze from the prairies,
Leaves on the aspen,
Mingle together,
Sing in the sunlight.

The following Shoshone-Bannock myth accounts for the creation of the lava field now known as the Craters of the Moon National Monument.

The Craters of the Moon

Long, long ago, a huge serpent, miles and miles in length, lay where the channel of the Snake River is now. Though the serpent was never known to harm anyone, people were terrified by it.

One spring, after it had lain asleep all winter, it left its bed and went to a large mountain in what is now the Craters of the Moon. There it coiled its immense body around the mountain and sunned itself.

After several days, thunder and lightning passed over the mountain and aroused the wrath of the serpent. A second time flashes of lightning played on the mountain, and this time the lightning struck nearby. Angered, the serpent began to tighten its coils around the mountain. Soon the pressure caused the rocks to begin to crumble.

Still the serpent tightened its coils. The pressure became so great that the stones began to melt. Fire came from the cracks. Soon liquid rock flowed down the sides of the mountains.

The huge serpent, slow in its movements, could not get away from the fire. So it was killed by the heat, and its body was roasted in the hot rock. At last the fire burned itself out; the rocks cooled off; the liquid rock became solid again.

Today if one visits the spot, he will see ashes and charred bones where the mountain used to be. If he will look closely at the solidified rock, he will see the ribs and bones of the huge serpent, charred and lifeless.

In the numerous Coyote stories common among most of the western tribes, Coyote, the trickster, is alternately victor and victim. In the following Shoshone story he is killed, but his death is a common motif, and he never stays dead for long.

Coyote and the Rock

Coyote was walking along the river when he came to a large white rock. Everyone was afraid of it, but Coyote walked right up to it and spat on it. Then he went away. After a while Coyote looked back and the rock seemed to be rolling after him.

Coyote thought, "That rock will never be able to catch me," so he ran along, making fun of the rock. At first he ran along the slope of a hill. The rock followed him. He went downhill again, and this time he was nearly caught. He ran through a narrow gorge, but the rock shattered the rocks in its way and continued the chase. Coyote crossed a stream. The rock plunged in and followed. Coyote went through a wood. The rock made a path for itself by knocking down all the trees. Coyote did not know what to do. The rock was just behind him, treading in his tail and heels.

The Coyote saw a Bear digging for wild carrots. "Aunt," he cried, "this rock is going to kill me, get behind me." The Bear stepped between them and stood up on her hind legs, but the rock knocked her to pieces. Coyote fled until he came to an Elk. "This rock is killing me," he cried. "Get behind me." The Elk got behind him, and raised his antlers against the rock, but the rock crushed him and went after Coyote.

Finally, Coyote came to a man who was building a fire. "Brother," he cried, "the rock is killing me." The man apparently paid no attention to Coyote, but when the rock approached, he just pushed out his elbow and hit it. The rock was shattered into small pieces. The man had large beads on his elbow, which formed his medicine, and it was this charm that killed the rock. Coyote fell to the ground, completely exhausted. After some time he arose, walked around the hill and killed the man by striking him with a stone. He then stole the charm and put it on his arm.

Coyote now walked uphill and got ready for a rock that

might tumble down. A rock began to roll down. As it
approached Coyote, he put out his elbow and it was split
asunder. "This is nothing," said Coyote. He went up
higher and waited for a bigger rock to tumble toward him.
The rock came down, but before Coyote had time to
stretch out his elbow, it crushed and killed him. Only his
tail stuck out beneath.

Dana Cassadore is a Northern Paiute who lives on the Duck Valley
reservation south of Boise on the Idaho-Nevada border.

DANA CASSADORE

The Tribal Artist

the parchment consumes the magic
        black liquid
as it spreads, it seeks each crevice
        caresses woven fibers
visions hold and multiply
voice of thoughts whispers
        strength to those who listen

there will be no death
        except in ignorance
in time, the pebble dropped
        into the collective well
will greet the water below
raising the level of the sky

Credence

a knowing grin echoes
as the night unfolds wings
stretched endless by time

a two faced warrior
finds game in the moon

rabbit hunts
where the scarecrow wades
the yellow ocean

a candle is carried by haunting winds
then hung in effigy

because i follow the raven
like the day longs to be night
and i watch the black pearl glisten

the beak holds the sweating message
waiting to be dropped in a dream

Coeur d'Alene

To represent the Coeur d'Alene tribal mythology, we have selected a short "water mystery" pertaining to local sites and a story about the "little people" or dwarfs, who are similar in nature to the Nez Perce "stick people." The Coeur d'Alene and such neighboring tribes as the Flatheads and the Kalispels spoke Salishan, while the Nez Perce spoke the Sahaptian dialect.

Lake Coeur d'Alene

At the mouth of the Coeur d'Alene River, there used to be a water mystery with the form of a buffalo. One time when a man was paddling along the lake shore in the dark, his canoe suddenly stood still. Though he paddled as hard as he could, the canoe did not move. He looked around him, in the water and on the shore. He could see nothing, so he paddled again. Still the canoe did not move.

The man felt along the bow of the boat and found that a horn was holding it on each side. Then he knew that the Water Buffalo had caught him. He put some beads on the horns and begged it to let him go. The buffalo settled back in the water, the canoe was freed, and the man paddled away.

Ever after, people left beads and other gifts on the bushes near that place and prayed to the water mystery not to harm them and not to make the lake windy.

The Little People

In the old days, many dwarfs lived around Rosebud Lake. It used to be surrounded by dense forest with much underbrush. Trees and bushes were so thick that people could get through them only with difficulty. That's the kind of place the dwarfs liked.

In the evenings my family would sometimes hear sticks beating against the trunks of trees. My grandparents would say, "The dwarfs are hitting the trees." We children would be afraid.

Sometimes people saw the Little People. Some people said that they wore brown suits with pointed brown caps. Others said that they were red all over and were dressed in red. They went up and down trees very quickly, always head first. In the trees, they walked with their feet on the under side of the branches, their heads hung down, but their caps were still on their heads. They carried their babies upside down on board carriers.

Sometimes people would be awakened suddenly by the crying of dwarfs in the night. They were a nuisance then, for they would wail and wail.

People approached by the dwarfs lost their senses, and when they came out of their stupor they found themselves leaning against a tree, upside down. Sometimes they missed part of their clothing and, on looking around, saw it hanging high up in the trees. Sometimes the dwarfs took food away and hid it. Sometimes they took bags of camas and tied them to the ends of branches of trees. But they never kept anything they had taken, and they never hurt anyone. They just liked to play tricks.

Dwarfs of another kind were about the size of small boys. They lived in cliffs and in rocky places in the mountains. In the old days, they were very numerous in the Coeur d'Alene and Nez Perce countries. They dressed in squirrel skins and used small bows and arrows. They often shouted when they saw people, and in this way often led hunters astray.

Janet Campbell Hale was born on the Coeur d'Alene reservation in Worley and lived on the Yakima reservation in Washington before going to California, where she received her B.A. from the University

of California at Berkeley and her M.A. from Davis. She presently
teaches at Western Washington University in Bellingham.

JANET CAMPBELL HALE/WORLEY

Backyard Swing

Did you ever
Swing in my swing
Behind our house
In Worley?
The house is still there
But the tree is gone.
My father made me
That swing,
You must remember—
The heavy rope
Tied around the
Sturdy branch,
Two of us could
Swing together.

Did you ever,
While way up high,
Close your eyes and drop
Your head way back,
Open eyes,
glimpse patches of sky
Through leafy branches,
Look at
Leaves, shimmering
green on one side,
Dull grey on the other,
Leaves shimmering
When the wind
Moved them?

You must remember
That tree and that swing.
The house is still there,
Windowless and stepless,
Without insides,
Groaning when the
Wind moves it.

Desmet, Idaho, March 1969

At my father's wake,
The old people
        Knew me,
    Though I
        Knew them not,
And spoke to me
In our tribe's
Ancient tongue,
Ignoring
The fact
That I
Don't speak
The language.
And so
I listened
As if I understood
What it was all about,
And,
Oh,
How it
Stirred me
To hear again
That strange
        Softly
        Flowing
Native tongue,
So
Familiar to
My childhood ear.

Kutenai

The Kutenai (sometimes spelled Kootenai) of the Idaho panhandle
are a small tribe whose dialect is distinct from that of the neighboring
Salishan-speaking peoples. Most tribes have myths of a flood or deluge, and we have selected one of these to represent the Kutenai,
along with a short sweatbath lyric.

The Deluge

One day Chicken-hawk's wife, Pheasant, went to pick
berries. About mid-day, tired and hot, she went down to

the lake for a bath. No sooner was she in the water than she saw Ya-woo-nik, a water-monster, and she was frightened. As she hurriedly swam to the shore, he called to her not to be frightened, for he was not going to harm her. Then she stopped, and he made love to her. She gave him all her berries, and remained with him until it was late. Afraid to go home without berries, she went to the mountains and hurriedly gathered some fruit, breaking off leaves and twigs in her haste. When she reached home, her husband asked at once why she had brought such berries, and she replied that she had had a headache and had not been able to gather clean fruit.

Chicken-hawk was suspicious, and on the next day he followed her. While she picked berries, she sang happily, and gathered clean fruit. About noon she had a great quantity and went to the lake, still gayly singing, and at the shore she threw the berries into the water. Chicken-hawk, keeping close in order to see what she was doing, beheld the monster coming through the water. Ya-woo-nik ate the berries, and Pheasant stood on the shore singing. Then she went into the water.

Chicken-hawk hastened home, to mend his arrows and to look after his bow. In the evening his wife returned again with trashy berries, and with her head bandaged, feigning headache. Chicken-hawk made no complaint.

On the next day he followed her again; saw her quickly gather berries and carry them to the lake; saw the monster eat them and then come ashore to caress her. At that moment Chicken-hawk put an arrow through his body. Water began to stream forth from the wound, and it spread and rose higher and higher. All creatures fled to the mountains, and Chicken-hawk put one of his tail-feathers into the ground to mark the rise of the water. When it reached the last stripe, it stopped and receded. Had it passed that mark, it would have destroyed them all.

Sweatbath Prayer

We here, the people, ask thee
rock and earth of the sweathouse
to bear our petitions to the sun, moon and stars
and through these to the Great Master Spirit.
Grant us food, wealth, health, shelter and care.

The Pioneer Poets
❦ *(1860–1900)*

Introduction

THE ROOTS OF IDAHO'S POETRY MAY BE FOUND IN NATIVE AMERIcan song (Nez Perce, Shoshone-Bannock, Coeur d'Alene), but Idaho's first poets in the conventional literary sense of the term were, in comparison to those roots, all tendrils. None were natives to the territory, most remain anonymous, and many were temporary residents, recording their infatuation with Idaho only so long as their luck held out in the gold mines. Most of the poems published during the territorial era and the early years of statehood appeared in newspapers, the majority of which were weeklies. The first newspaper in the territory, the *Golden Age*, started up in Lewiston on 2 August 1862. With the *Boise News*, the *Idaho World* (Idaho City), and the *Owyhee Avalanche* (Silver City), the *Golden Age* aired the literary aspirations and flirtations of Idaho's first "published" poets.

Literary tastes have changed to such a degree that to some readers the poems of Idaho's late-nineteenth-century versifiers, who assumed such fanciful monikers as Log-Cabin, Pay Rock, Vaquero, and Grey Eagle, may sound as foreign as the translated Native American songs. Tennyson was poet laureate in England at the time, and America's favorites were the "Fireside Poets"—Henry Wadsworth Longfellow (1807–1882), John Greenleaf Whittier (1807–1892), and Oliver Wendell Holmes (1809–1904). The poets of that era who are most often, the focus of American literature courses today, Walt Whitman and Emily Dickinson, had little or no popular reputation. Metrically, the amateur poets of Idaho's gold rush and early settlement days were cautiously conservative, favoring simple couplets or alternating rhyme schemes with the ballad stanza being most popular, as in Sarah Huckvale's "Bear Lake" (1883):

> Bear Lake forever!
>   Our watchword shall be:
> Our Home in the mountains,
>   Unfettered and free.

Thematically, too, the poems reflect the limited complexity and depth, not simply of another supposedly simpler era, but of the amateur writer who has only a limited understanding of his or her craft. Nostalgia and sentimentality combine with glorification of the picturesque in nature, as in G.E.B.'s "The Wild Forget-Me-Nots of Owyhee" (1890):

> On each slanting ridge sweeping up from below,
> In each rocky dell, warm with spring's rosy glow,
> The sturdy Forget-Me-Not's violet crest
> Invites the brown bees in its calyx to rest.

Although they are not represented here, by far the largest number of poems printed in Idaho's early newspapers were memorial verses of the most banal variety. The following anonymous quatrain from the *Lewiston Teller* (1880) represents both the clichéd sentiments of these painful poems, which are, after all, sincere statements of grief and attempts at consolation, and the limited metrical control:

> No more around the social hearth
>   Thou hear'st her pleasant voice—
> She was too pure for earth
>   And so the angels took her home.

There are times with poetry when sincerity of feeling alone is not enough.

For our selections we have favored poems that reflect the poet's awareness of place and those that capture aspects of character which might be seen as "distinctive" (Western, at least, if not specifically Idahoan) and are often humorous. The homespun poets of the Idaho Territory frequently seem less bound by convention, more willing to test their own "voice" when they are not serious. They are most apt to sound stilted, artificial, or imitative when they are moralizing or philosophizing, as in the following lines of consolation from Z.Z. in the *Idaho World* (1878):

> Soon your soul will cease its sorrow;
>   Soon a heaven it will gain
> Where no care will mar its quiet
>   Or no trouble give it pain.

The responses of Idaho's early poets to the rugged but beautiful land they had come to, often to gouge for gold, varied from awe to adoration. George P. Wheeler's "Idaho Retrospective" (1886), published in the *Caldwell Tribune*, reflects upon miles of "sun-scorched earth," a "treeless waste," "A mighty empire, desolate,/Untaught by Progress' guiding hand." But he anticipates a bright future for the territory, a "glittering dawn" of the sort that seems to have inspired an anonymous New Year's poem more than twenty years before. Early in that poem "Log-Cabin" reflects upon "Yon snowy mountains stretch'd around," a sagebrush fire, and wolves howling outside, but he concludes as follows: "The struggle's past. With ray serene/The empire star all-girds the scene,/I'm satisfied, I must repeat" (*Boise News*, 1864). One of the more unusual celebrations of place is H. F. Johnson's "Farewell to Idaho" (1895), which half admires the "civilizing magic wand" that has transformed the young state and half laments the passing of "the primal plain:/Where roamed the savage beasts of prey." Johnson concludes first with a "farewell" to "Her clear and sparkling streams,/Her mountains robed in purest snow," then breaks off and announces that he spoke too soon and, having "struck it rich," has decided to settle down.

Of a very different nature from the sometimes rhapsodic, even promotional praise of Idaho's scenic grandeur are poems that offer us such characters as "The Rustic Miner," who has no use for anyone unused to hard work, or the "grumpy old bachelor" who just wants the spinsters and widows to leave him alone. In "The 'Bad Man' from the Range" (1890), George P. Wheeler, who served as Speaker in the Idaho House of Representatives, offers a comic narrative poem that may remind some readers of Robert Service's Yukon tales.

> "Barkeep, set 'em up!" yelled Peter,
> "Set 'em up, you lean muskeeter!"
> And he pulled his big repeater,
>   And he spit upon the floor.
> "Don't you see I'm wild and Wooly?
> Don't you see I'm feelin' bully?
> Fill the glasses, fill 'em fully;
>   Don't you see I yearn for gore?"

In compiling the poems for this section of the anthology, we have been well aware that the work has at best marginal literary merit. These poems do constitute a sort of "literary heritage," however, and they are appropriately classified as the products of "pioneer" poets. Every state of the union very likely has a similar number of lost poets of the nineteenth century, and most of their work no doubt deserves the quiet oblivion that has settled on it. We are content here to rescue these few poems, if only temporarily, for what they tell of the attitudes, values, hopes, and dreams of Idaho's first literary figures.

The Pioneer Poets

LOG-CABIN *Boise News*, 16 January 1864

A New Year View of the World Inside and Out

Around remembered hearth-stones dear,
From blooming youth to old in year,
   How many hearts beat high for joy!
A sage brush flame my heat and light,
I'm sitting here alone to-night,
   And doggerel rhymes my mind employ.

A million bonfires blazing high,
Ten thousand guns that rend the sky,
   Proclaim this day earth's jubilee:—
Yon snowy mountains stretch'd around,
The wolves whose howls their wilds resound,
   Are all that I can hear or see.

The New Year dinners served, how rare!
What streams of wine to wash off care
   Have sparkled bright the wide world o'er!—
With flap-jacks dry and bear meat fried,
Log-cabin has been satisfied;
   His pure wine flows right past his door.

This day old feuds are cast aside—
The fickle friends are multiplied—
   The social jars forgotten are.
My nearest friend, "across the way,"
(The distance twenty miles they say,)
   And I have never split a hair.

I guess outsiders all will say
A chap's a fool to live this way,
   And think my lot extremely hard.
Let people think just what they please;
Log-cabin's mind is quite at ease—
   He soon will meet a just reward.

E'en now methinks before my eyes
The great results in grand splendor rise
   That pioneers look forward to:
The wolf and panther are no more;
Domestic herds yon hills are o'er;
   Behold what homesteads meet the view!

Thro' vales, Payette and Boise glide
When church and school house, side by side,
   Attest the people's moral tone;
In a worldly view, on ev'ry hand,
The horn of plenty fills the land—
   The harvest pioneers had sown.

Those clustered roofs that now appear,
Whence comes this din that fills the ear,
   Of art and commerce are the seat.
The struggle's past. With ray serene
The empire star all-girds the scene,
   I'm satisfied, I must repeat.

A.J./BUENA VISTA BAR *Idaho World*, 18 February 1865

Our Cabin on the Bar

From stranger dwellings distant wide,
   'Mid sturdy, towering pines,
Where thick stand cabins side by side,
   Now o'er the golden mines—
Scarce two moons since, in coy retreat,
   Far from the crowd and jar,
We reared, in wood retirement sweet,
   Our cabin on the bar.

And from our six-paned window here,
   O'erlooking vale and town,
We watch in moonlight calm and clear,
   The dancing stars go down;
All crested o'er with silver dew,
   High heav'nward shining far,
Proud mountain tops look down to view
   Our cabin on the bar.

Far, far removed from older friends,
  Wide desert plains between,
Rude strangeness here enchantment lends
  The rugged mountain scene:
Though long loved ones do nevermore
  To cheer us here afar,
Strange though it seem, indeed we love
  Our cabin on the bar.

Our genial fire-place blazing bright,
  Lights no vindictive sheet
All reeking with invectives blight,
  Our saddened gaze to meet:
All teeming with envenomed taunt,
  And tales of brothers' war,
Malignant papers rarely haunt
  Our cabin on the bar.

Here sit we by our fireside light,
  In savage peaceful clime,
Far from the enlightened, Christian fight,
  The beauty of the time:
Highwaymen ne'er with civil gun—
  To drag us off to war—
Demand our cash or life, within
  Our cabin on the bar.

Fresh, steaming dailies never come,
  Crammed with conflicting lies,
To fret us in our mountain home
  'Neath Idahoan skies;
Of bar'brous men, bedyed in sin,
  Who hated bloody war.
E'er peace were treason, we read, in
  Our cabin on the bar.

When new-made friends do gather near
  Our footlight's gladsome ray,
With orient tales of homeland cheer,
  At quiet close of day:
Each in his turn, his yarn to spin,
  Like some seafaring tar,
Loud rings the merry laughter in
  Our cabin on the bar.

With all arranged for bachy ease,
    Apartments all combined,
Where starch conventionalities
    Their elements ne'er find—
"Housework done up" with slighting strike,
    Our things pitched here and "thar,"
We wonder, would our sweethearts like
    Our cabin on the bar?

When we our wayward footsteps turn
    Homeward, in future years,
To quiet anxious friends' concern,
    'Mid joyful smiles and tears,
Our lingering thoughts will often dwell
    Where we now musing are,
We'll evermore remember well
    Our cabin on the bar.

ANONYMOUS/IDAHO CITY *Boise News*, 21 March 1864

To M.V.E.

When present scenes have passed away,
    And youth's bright days have flown,
Do not forget these sincere words,—
    "Amiga de mi Corazon."

When other lips repeat thy name
    With soft and tender tone,
Remember how I love that sound—
    "Amiga de mi Corazon."

Or when lamenting o'er some grief
    In silence and alone,
Remember thou'lt be then as now—
    "Amiga de mi Corazon."

SCOTTISH CHIEF/SILVER CITY *Owyhee Avalanche,*
14 November 1865

Poor Man

On Oro Fino's towering heighths,
Where storms delight to play,
A poor man bold, in search of gold,
Plod on his weary way.

Beneath him wide, on ev'ry side,
Spread lava plains beyond,
Reminding him of fifteen years,
All vainly spent and gone.

Though nought in purse, and illy clad,
Hope's fires still burn'd within;
With steady tread he press'd ahead,
Determin'd yet to win.

The wint'ry blasts unheeded pass'd
Him on his tramp that day,
Whilst dreams of gems and diadems,
Kept death and want at bay.

Hope's phantom lights, a thousand nights
Before, had round him spread;
The silver bricks, with diamonds mix'd—
A wide and downy bed.

As thus he roam'd o'er crag and height,
No care to live a day,
A something bright burst on his sight,
Billions around him lay!

Owyhee bare! before him stood
There, in the glare of day,
Bedeck'd with gems and diadems,
And charms that ne'er decay.

The poor man bold, in search of gold,
Th' dev'l in his eyes, d'ye see?
Pitch'd in to win—and was not sold
On Miss O. Owyhee.

From Webfoot's shores to Utah's plains,
Now the poor man's luck is known,
And wealth in piles, and women's smiles,
Are his—*whilst he holds his own.*

PAY ROCK *Idaho Weekly Avalanche,* 29 January 1876

The Owyhee Miner's Lament

Good-bye, old Owyhee, I'm going to the States;
Your mining population have got to emigrate,
'Cause the Bulls and Bears of 'Frisco, with
    their pocket full of dimes,
Have played the very devil with all our leading
    mines.

   Chorus—Rip, rap, flip flap,
   I wish I had my money back;
   I would deal no more 'n mining stocks—
   I would be a wiser man.

Oh! there's the Ida Ellmore, the Poorman, and the
    Pauper,
With their assessments I'm dead broke, I haven't
    got a quarter;
They kept sinking and drifting all around the
    lower levels,
Till I'm dead broke, my coat's in soak, and I'm
    going to the Devil.

   Chorus—Rip, rap, etc.

Some time ago Mahogany was thought to be a buy,
A few hundred I invested again my luck to try;
I kept watching and waiting expecting a big rise,
When a two-dollar assessment it opened wide my eyes.

   Chorus—Rip, rap, etc.

There's the Oro Fino, the pride of all the camp.
But, when she failed to come to time, it caused the
    boys to tramp

With their blankets on their shoulders from morning
    until noon,
Since the Superintendant went to 'Frisco and flopped
    the big Muldoon.

    Chorus—Rip, rap, etc.

Oh! once I had money plenty enough to buy a farm.
But to take a deal in mining stocks I thought 'twould
    be no harm.
So five thousand I invested in Golden Charlot stock,
When all at once she took a flop—they couldn't find
payrock.

    Chorus—Rip, rap, etc.

DARBY *Idaho Avalanche*, 11 August 1877

The Rustic Miner

My home is on the mountain tops,
    My bed's among the willows,
I envy not the lazy fops
    Who lounge on downy pillows;
What care I for a city life,
    There's not to me seems finer
Than to be free from crowded strife
    And be a rustic miner.

Let farmers prate of cows and bulls,
    And soldiers talk of fighting,
And sailors sing cross-yards and hulls,
    And lawyers live by writing;
But I'll not swap for any trade
    From Governor down to joiner,
Of hard work I was ne'er afraid
    For I'm a rustic miner.

And when the sun with radiant hue
    Peeps o'er the eastern mountains,
To quaff the morning's glistening dew,
    And gild the rippling fountains,
I'm at my work with all my might,
    In search of the "glittering shiner";

Ah! where's the man that's more upright
    Than the hardy, rustic miner?

He cares not for the tyrant whelp;
    To treachery he's a stranger;
His friend and foe alike he'll help
    When either are in danger.
He trusts in God, in Him alone,
    He sees the great assigner;
Though every hope on earth be gone,
    God loves the rustic miner.

Then who would starve, and pine, and rot,
    Within a murky city?
While on these hills there's many a spot
    Where gold abounds; oh what a pity
These growling, lazy, crawling elves,
    Known to all men as whiners,
Would not step out and help themselves,
    And work like honest miners.

G.E.B. *Idaho Avalanche*, 10 May 1890

The Wild Forget-Me-Nots of Owyhee

The pale crystal sheaves of the storm-garnered snow
Have shrunk from the kiss of the sun's ardent glow,
And, in bright, pearly tears of dissolving delight,
Have melted and flowed far away out of sight.

The high-crested snow-waves, all frozen and fair,
Have ebbed from the hill-tops and left the earth bare;
While now, 'mid the dead stalks that blossomed last year,
The tender, green leaflets and grass-blades appear.

The dark, granite ribs of the bleak mountain side
Lie gaunt, bare and warm in the mellow springtide,
And the silver-gray coat of the sagebrush is seen,
New-tipped with a fringe of faint, delicate green.

'Tis a wave of a wand,—scarce the flight of a day.—
Ere green robes are flung o'er the hill's tawny gray,
While high mounts the new wine of spring in the blood
Of insect and leaflet, of flower and wood.

39

The soft, curling grasses, with feathery plume,
Are slowly unfurling in summer's first bloom.
And velvet-winged butterflies seek the wild rose
Where swift, by the willows, the trout-brook flows.

On each slanting ridge sweeping up from below,
In each rocky dell, warm with spring's rosy glow,
The sturdy Forget-Me-Not's violet crest
Invites the brown bees in its calyx to rest.

Its cup from the sky catches tints of deep blue,
And steals from the day-dawn its pearliest hue;
It bathes in the pink of the crimson twilight,
And gleams through the sedges like stars of the night.

'Tis Owyhee's fair jewel, her crown and her pride,
Where purple it flames on each steep mountain side;
And the gold in her granite-browed hills is less fair
Than the dainty Forget-Me-Nots blossoming there.

SARAH HUCKVALE/BEAR LAKE *Bear Lake Democrat*,
24 March 1883

Bear Lake

Bear lake forever!
   Our watchword shall be:
Our Home in the mountains,
   Unfettered and free.

Where foot of white man
   But seldom has trod,
We came and we prospered
   All alone with our God.

Here long we have dwelt
   In safety and peace,
Unharmed by the billows
   Of war or distress;

We've minded our work
   We've quarreled with none;

Then why can't outsiders
   Please to let us alone?

The pathway of right
   We'll travel along,
With Bear Lake for ever!
   The chorus of our song.

GEORGE P. WHEELER *Idaho World*, 7 February 1890

The 'Bad Man' from the Range

Bronch Pete he was a dandy,
Though he had a taste for brandy.
With his gun he was quite handy,
   In a melancholy way.
He could outswear any swearer;
On the range he was a rearer.
Big and bold, he was a terror,
   Like a buffalo at play.

And he scorned the bashful stranger,
And he mocked him, this wild ranger,
And he told him of his danger
   In the wild and wooly west.
Then he yanked him by the shoulder,
By his actions then made bolder;
Swore they'd "likker" 'fore they're older;
   Got a tenderfoot out west.

"Barkeep, set 'em up!" yelled Peter,
"Set 'em up, you lean muskeeter!"
And he pulled his big repeater,
   And he spit upon the floor.
"Don't you see I'm wild and Wooly?
Don't you see I'm feelin' bully?
Fill the glasses, fill 'em fully;
   Don't you see I yearn for gore?"

"Don't ye see my blood is bilin'?
Don't ye see for gore I'm spilin'?
Fer a fight I'm quickly rilin';
   I'm a catbird; I'm a brick!

I'm a terror, I'm er snorter!
Betcher life—or else you'd orter!
I'm from the extreme headwater
    Of the stream called Bittercreek!"

Swiftly then the stranger grabbed him,
With his fist he quickly dabbed him,
Fiercely in the eye he jabbed him,
    Wallowed him upon the floor.
And the tenderfoot he jumped him,
Bumped and pumped and soundly thumped him,
Out of doors he gently dumped him—
    Dumped the man who bathed in gore.

Then the little man of muscle
Who had won the mighty tussle,
Who had conquered with his rustle
    In the gay and gallant fight,
Said no doubt he could be rougher,
But he thought the chap was tougher;
"Gentlemen, I am the duffer
    Who will box for you tonight,"

Anonymous *Nez Perce News*, 26 October 1882

The Candidate

The politician, smooth and bland,
    Has many winning ways,
And to and fro throughout the land
    He travels all his days.

A modest man, of modest ends,
    He runs reluctantly;
He's ever forced, by certain friends,
    A candidate to be.

It injures much his business
    To be a public func;
For oftentimes, while under stress,
    He getteth beastly drunk.

He speaks a piece to every man,
  However low and rude;
Much takes he from newspapers, and
  Much is a platitude.

The beer to drink, the babes to kiss,
  He hastily doth pass;
Among the agriculturalists
  He tramples down the grass.

He asks, with earnest bend of head,
  After your family,
And be they sick, or well, or dead,
  Never a curse cares he.

ARION *Idaho World*, 8 August 1874

Advice to Beaux

I would caution the ardent swains
  That wait upon ladies fair,
Not with hasty upbraiding strains
  Or a sanctimonious air,
But with good and wholesome advice
  When taken—It always suits,
It is neither stylish, nor gallant nor nice
  "To wear your pants in your boots."
When calling upon your "choice,"
  Or acting as an escort,
Let appearance, manner and voice
  Be everything that they ought,
—Unless wading through Webfoot mud,—
  Like other unlucky Coots,
Or, looking again for Noah's flood,
  "Don't wear your pants in your boots."

You, handsome as an Apollo;
  Your language very precise,
Find it your interest to follow
  My seemingly rude advice,
For that facetious god "Cupid"
  No love-feathered arrow shoots
For any swain that's so stupid
  As to court—with his pants in his boots.

VAQUERO *Idaho Recorder*, 8 October 1887

To "Sally Cactus"

Now, Sally dear, you've broke me up
With your little sausage grinder!
The Junction widow has decamped
And darned if I can find her.
I did intend to marry her
Before the winter closes,
And take her down to Florida
To live among the roses.
But life is short, I turn to you
For love and consolation.
Tell me, can I make a match?
Have you any inclination
To wed, with one whose heart is full
Of love and tender passion?
Now, tell me true, and do not fool,
For that is out of fashion.
Your name implies you're full of thorns,
But love will dangers run.
If you say yes, I'll tackle you—
Although I have but one.
Now, Sally, if it is a whack,
I'll shake the widow lady;
We'll run away to Florida—
Yes, you can take the baby.

ANONYMOUS/BOONVILLE *Idaho Avalanche*, 28 March 1885

Country Girls

Up in the morning early—
   Just at the peep of day—
Straining the milk in the dairy,
   Turning the cows away,
Sweeping the floor in the kitchen,
   Making the beds upstairs,
Washing the breakfast dishes,
   Dusting the parlor chairs,

Brushing crumbs from the pantry,
   Hunting for eggs in the barn,
Cleaning turnips for dinner,
   Spinning stocking yarn,
Spreading the whitened linen
   Down on the bushes below,
Ransacking every meadow
   Where the red strawberries grow,
Starching the fixtures for Sunday,
   Churning the snowy cream,
Rinsing the pail and strainer
   Down in the limpid stream.
Feeding the geese and turkeys,
   Making the pumpkin pies,
Jogging young one's cradle,
   Driving away the flies;
Grace in every motion,
   Music in every tone.
Beauty in form and feature—
   Thousands may covet to own—
Cheeks that rival spring roses,
   Teeth the whitest of pearl;
One of these country maids
   Is worth a score of your city girls.

ANONYMOUS/BOISE *Idaho Tri-Weekly Statesman,*
30 November 1880

A Bachelor's Growl

I'm a grumpy old bachelor,
   Grizzly and gray.
I am seven-and-forty
   If I am a day.
I am fussy and crusty,
   And dry as a bone,
So ladies—good ladies—
   Just let me alone!

Go shake out your ringlets,
   And beam out in smiles,

Go tinkle your trinkets
  And show off your wiles.
Bewitch and bewilder
  Wherever you can;
But pray—pray, remember,
  I am not the man!

I'm frozen to blushes,
  I'm proof against eyes;
I'm hardened to simpers
  And stony to sighs;
I'm tough to each dart
  That young Cupid can lance;
I'm not in the market
  At any advance!

I sew my own buttons,
  I darn my own hose,
I keep my own counsel
  And fold my own clothes.
I mind my own business
  And live my own life;
I won't —no, the Dickens—
  Be plagued with a wife.

And yet there's nine spinsters
  Who believe me their fate;
There's two dozen widows
  Who'd change their estate;
There's silly young maidens
  Who blush at my bow;
All—all bent on marrying me,
  No matter how!

I walk forth in trembling;
  I come home in dread;
I don't fear my heart,
  But I do fear my head!
My civilest speech
  Is a growl and a nod;
And that—Heaven save me!—
  Is "charmingly odd!"

So ladies—dear ladies—
    Just hear me, I pray,
I speak to you all
    In the pluralest way;
My logic is simple
    As logic can be—
If I won't marry you,
    Pray—don't marry me!

GREY EAGLE *Boise News*, 20 August 1864

Up Goes Idaho

I'm standing now upon a hill
That looks down on the town,
I'm thinking of that mighty will
Which never can bow down;
I mean the will of Enterprise
That made our nation grow,
And from these Indian wilds built up
The town of Idaho.

For, lo! the silent Indian trod
Alone in savage pride,
Not four years since, upon this sod,
Where now but whites reside;
This could not be his resting place,
For Enterprise said, go!
The red man turned to leave the land,
And up goes Idaho.

Not many years ahead I look—
Where is the red man now?
Not found beside the murmuring brook,
But gone, and none know where;
First leaving one sequestered spot,
And then one more, when lo!
The white man calls the land his own—
The red man's Idaho.

A few more years the telegraph
And rushing cars proclaim,

How feeble is the red man's wrath,
Should he come back again;
While rushing tides are beating on,
Still further must he go,
Until he makes his hunting ground
Far, far from Idaho.

GEORGE P. WHEELER *Caldwell Tribune*, 15 May 1886

Idaho Retrospective

Mile upon mile of sun-scorched earth;
    Mile upon mile of desert plain;
A treeless waste, scarce trod by man;
    A wilderness unblessed with rain,

A cloudless sky—a blazing sun;
    A solitude wild, vast, profound;
An empire strange and unexplored;
    An empire girt about, around,

By mountain ranges reared aloft,
    Their snow-clad summits towering high,
Like sturdy warriors of old,
    Against a dazzling summer sky.

Far to the north, the Teton Range,
    Grim sentinels, their vigils keep;
Their crested heads eternal snow;
    While the vast plain is wrapped in sleep.

A sleep unbroken; for, as yet,
    The savage warrior roams at will,
The wild deer and the antelope
    Alone the trackless desert fill.

Mile upon mile of arid waste;
    Mile upon mile of glaring sand;
A mighty empire, desolate,
    Untaught by Progress' guiding hand;

Circled and girt about, around,
    By hoary mountains, capped in snow,

Awaken thou! the scene has changed.
  Shake off thy slumber, Idaho!

A hardy race of pioneers,
  Valiant and brave, like giants rude,
Have burst upon thee from afar,
  Have pierced thy pristine solitude.

Thy arid wastes are made to smile
  And yield their tribute to the might
Of sinewy hands; a brighter dawn
  Bursts forth and banishes the night.

Where once the Indian, wild and free,
  Rode forth at dawn beneath the skies,
To join the chase in savage glee,
  Cities and villages arise;

While Nature, 'neath the soft caress,
  Where all was wilderness before,
Beams o'er the land in gratitude,
  And gladly yields her bounteous store.

And far away, remote from all,
  Amid the mountain summits bold,
She smiles again on other hands,
  And empties forth her hoarded gold.

And from the East the iron horse
  Bursts upon thee in his might;
Of Progress he the messenger;
  A flashing meteor of light.

Arouse thee, Idaho! Shake off
  Thy slumbers! Scatter hence the shade!
Awaken to the glittering dawn
  Of thy great future, ne'er to fade!

And may that future be as bright
  As thy own birthplace 'mid the snow,
Success, prosperity, be thine,
  "Gem of the Mountains," Idaho!

Naomi McDonald Phelps *Daily Statesman*, 30 May 1890

A Mountain Idyl

Beyond me lies
The Mountains' massive chain.
Their brows uplifted and their huge arms bare,
That reaching upward, clasp the middle air
As though to twine about their foreheads fair,
From fleecy skies
The vapors' misty train.

The purple tide
Of distance rolls between.
And yet their rugged heights in martial rows
(Rim'd with diadems of last year's snows)
Stand in their sorted ranks that yet disclose
About each rugged site,
The pines unfading green.

And many a yawning rent
Where leaping currents dashed;
When from their mountain caves the tempests spoke
And answering voices answered, till awoke
The spirit of the storms, that fiercely broke
Above the pines low bent,
And vivid lightnings flashed.

About their foreheads, where
To-day the white robes rest;
Of fleecy clouds whose flowery mist
By summer suns to glory kissed,
Of purple rose and amethyst,
That shines in beauty rare,
Each worn and storm-scarred breast.

The monuments of God,
Whose years are still untold;
And on their hoary summits rock o'erstrewn
The winged winds, upon whose breath is blown
The summer's incense rear their regal throne
(Where foot of man ne'er trod,
In eager search for gold.)

Or builds the massive walls
Of ice and snow,
Whose opalescent bulwarks waste away
When southwest winds through mountain gorges stray,
And summer snows wake with the drowsy day;
To loose the waterfalls,
Whose rhythmic flow their weepings swell.

Until in sullen wrath
They overflow all barriers; ploughing deep
The seams and rents along the frowning steep.
And downward plunge with wild resonant leap
To many a mountain dell,
While from their path

The puny weeds are tossed
As on with foam and hiss,
Their waters hasten to the drowthy plain,
To gladden all the desert, then again
Mix with the floods that seek the western main
Their crystal wavelets lost
In ocean's dark abyss.

Oh monuments of might
Scarred by the century's wars,
Behold how feeble and how little worth
Are the vast structures reared by sons of earth.
Compared with these hoar ghosts of primeval birth
Who bathed in ambient light,
Sang with the morning stars.

CLARENCE E. EDDY (1874–?) IN *Pinnacle of Parnassus* (1902)

Springtime in Idaho

Springtime out in Idaho,
All things come to him who waits;
We'd have you know that we can show
Just as much as other states:

Now the festive Thomas-cat
Warbles on the back yard fence,
And the wifie's new spring hat,
Causes hubby great expense;

Now the "yearlings blindly bleat,"
    And the flowers begin to bloom,
And the Weary Willies's feet
    Now their wanderings will resume.

Politicians now begin
    Figgerin' round in Idaho,
Both sides are a goin' to win;
    This is campaign year, you know.

Bullfrogs croakin' in the spring,
    How their music does remind us,
Of the songs they used to sing,
    In the land we left behind us.

Yaller dawg a yappin' an'
    Goodness gracious, see him sail,
Got a big termater can,
    Tightly tied on to his tail.

Dudes a lookin' stunnin' in
    Loudest kind o' pantaloons,
Idlers out a sunnin' in
    Front o' all o' the saloons.

Farmers finishing their crop,
    Though they never crop a whisker.
Price o' wheat may take a drop;
    Plant her, anyhow, and risk her.

Then we have the mines, you see,
    And we soon will have the "dough."
Bet yer life there's goin' to be
    "A hot time" here in Idaho.

Thunder Mountain mines, you know,
    There's a heap o' talk about,
Every town in Idaho
    Has the only natural route.

Men are gittin' grub and tools;
    Some for money, some on trust;

Loadin' it upon the mules—
  Thunder Mountain now or bust.

Yes, the spring at last is here,
  From the mountains melts the snow,
Goin' to be a glorious year
  For the State of Idaho.

H. F. JOHNSON (1830–1916)

The Israelite's Last Mule Ride

It was in the month of August,
  A summer month I believe,
When farmers all in Idaho
  Were gathering in their sheaves
Of golden grain to bless the land
  With nature's bounteous store,
And hunger, poverty and want
  To banish from our shore.

An Israelite came from the north,
  Of royal blood I believe,
But of the fact I am not sure,
  Appearances will deceive,
He landed at Salubria,
  From there he thought to ride
To where the miners sturdy strokes
  Had cleaved the mountain side.

He looked around, he found a beast,
  'Twas gentle, kind and true,
An eighty year old donkey
  He thought would take him through;
A mighty sum of gold he paid
  Then did the mule bestride,
And with his whip and spurs outdid
  John Gilpin's famous ride.

At Council Valley, on the route,
  His royal suite to cheer,

He turned his pockets wrong side out
  And bought some lager beer,
Then onward still he held his way
  Till night her mantle spread.
Then filled his royal carcass up
  With milk and went to bed.

The poor old donkey could not boast
  Of any surplus fat,
As on his hip, it's very plain,
  A man could hang his hat.
But still he popped the donkey through,
  And back to town he came,
Upon the donkey's hurricane deck
  He gained a world of fame.

King David rode upon a mule,
  And Christ upon an ass,
And here in Idaho we've found
  Their prototype at last;
The only difference I can see
  Against the ancient rule,
In modern times it came to be
  The ass should ride the mule.

Somehow I think, the story goes,
  That since that fearful ride
The poor old donkey sought repose
  In death by suicide.
He could not bear the keen rebuke;
  Of honor thus bereft,
He sought a deep and shady brook
  And found relief in death.

But if the story is untrue,
  The donkey still survives,
I hope they'll turn him on the range
  And let the hero thrive.
For if he takes that trip again
  For Israelitic gold,
May the great God that rules above
  Have mercy on his soul.

Farewell to Idaho

Come all ye heroes of the land,
   We'll sing of Western life,
Ye pioneers who led the van
   Through danger, toil and strife:
Who planted freedom's starry flag,
   In spite of savage foe,
Upon the rugged mountain peaks
   And plains of Idaho.

You saw the land in days of yore,
   When savage foes were 'round:
You heard, through valley, cove and dell,
   The warwhoop's dismal sound:
You've scaled her lofty mountain peaks,
   You've crossed the torrents arch,
You've met the grizzly in his path,
   The warrior on the march.

The wild deer bounded from his lair,
   And sped across the land:
The elk, that noblest beast of chase,
   Were seen on every hand:
The cougar's savage growl was heard,
   The gray wolf's dismal howl,
The coyote's yelping on the plain,
   Made music for us all.

The scene has changed: alas, no more
   The wild deer scuds the plain,
The lordly elk, a sylvan god,
   With us but few remain;
Our savage foeman, once so strong,
   Is feeble now at best,
His star of empire, once so grand,
   Is setting in the West.

We will see no more the trapper's day,
   The hunter's fame is gone,
The game and fur have passed away,
   No more can they return:

But in their stead domestic life
  Is teeming on the hills,
The lowing herds and tinkling bells,
  The air with music fills.

The civilizing magic wand
  Has touched the primal plain:
Where roamed the savage beasts of prey
  Now waves the golden grain;
Where stood the dusky warrior's lodge
  The school house proudly stands,
Where rose the savage warrior's cry
  The songs of peace ascend.

Where, in the mountain's solitude,
  Was heard but nature's song,
The miner's pick and anvil's-ring
  The chorus still prolong;
The mountains yield their precious store
  To beautify the land;
While labor, toil and enterprise
  Is seen on every hand.

While some have reached the golden shore,
  And dwell in fairy land,
Some struggle on with hope's bright star
  Still shining in the van;
While some beneath the churchyard sleep,
  Some rest in unknown graves,
Some met the storm king on the deep,
  And sleep beneath the waves.

To those who reached the golden shore
  By the just and honest way,
May peace and plenty crown their board,
  Till life shall pass away;
To those who struggle on in hope
  We give a hearty cheer;
To those who sleep in unknown graves
  We drop a friendly tear.

And now farewell to Idaho,
  Her clear and sparkling streams,

Her mountains robed in purest snow,
  Her valleys clothed in green;
'Tis fate's decree that I must go,
  And to my fate I yield;
I'll call and see you all again
  When fortune turns the wheel. . . .

That is the way I used to sing,
  But now I've changed my tune,
My talk of leaving Idaho
  Was a little bit too soon:
Dame Fortune smiled, I've struck it rich,
  And the best thing I can do
Is change my mind, and settle down,
  And see the country through.

Poets of a New State
✸ (1900–1940)

Introduction

ONE OF THE QUESTIONS HEARD MOST FREQUENTLY FROM PEOPLE
"in the know" is whether Vardis Fisher, Idaho's most renowned novelist, wrote any poems. He did, mostly sonnets, and we have included a few in this section of our anthology. We have not included
work from his sequence *Sonnets to an Imaginary Madonna* (1927),
but we have selected from the "Antelope People" sonnets, which
appeared in periodicals during the twenties and thirties.

Probably the second most commonly asked question was whether we
were going to include anything by Idaho's most famous literary native
son, Ezra Pound, who left the state at about eighteen months of age,
never to return. The question was sometimes phrased, "You're not
going to include Pound, are you?" Aside from a brief correspondence
with Senator Borah, Pound's writings are virtually devoid of refer-
ence to Idaho. But there are stories to the effect that Pound liked to
tease his cosmopolitan friends about being from Idaho, and when his
daughter visited the University of Idaho to receive an honorary degree in 1978, she reported that he had sometimes expressed a wish to
be buried in his native state. But in answer to the question, we have
included one of Pound's more accessible poems, one that is not often
anthologized, *Moeurs Contemporaines* ("Contemporary Manners"),
which appeared in *Lustra* (1915). We decided to print the poem
without notes because the few passages in French and Italian are
easily accessible; however, we feel obligated to inform those who
have been so good as to read this introduction that the massive Greek
word in the sixth section of the poem, "polu-phlois-boious," means
"loud-roaring," and the line of Greek in the text is a Homeric refer-
ence to the "loud-roaring sea." The Latin that follows means "Stay
traveler."

Other choices were less problematic. We are indebted to Professor
Jo Ann Ruckman, of the Idaho State University history department,
for passing along the poems of Annie Pike Greenwood, whose book,
We Sagebrush Folks, has been reissued by the University of Idaho
Press. And of course we wanted to represent the work of Idaho's first
poet laureate, Irene Welch Grissom, appointed by Governor C. C.
Moore in 1923. In preparing this section we were greatly assisted by

the pioneering anthology work of Bess Foster Smith's *Sunlit Peaks* (1931), published by Caxton Press in Caldwell.

In fact, many of our selections for this portion of the anthology are fortuitous. We knew that the renowned literary scholar, Yvor Winters, had taught in the foreign languages department at the University of Idaho for a couple years in the 1920s, so it was simply a matter of finding poems among his published work that reflected upon his stay in Idaho. We surmised that Moscow novelist Carol Ryrie Brink had written poems as well, and we found a few in *Poetry* dating back to the twenties, but Mary Reed of the Latah County Historical Society revealed some more recent work, which we reprint here through the courtesy of Mrs. Brink's daughter and son, Nora Hunter and David R. Brink.

Among our most interesting discoveries are the *avant garde* poems of a Weiser native, Forrest Anderson, whose modernist style is reminiscent of Hart Crane, to whom one of his poems is dedicated. A merchant seaman, Anderson lived in Paris in the 1930s and associated with Louis Zukofsky and other poets of the Objectivist movement. To encounter Anderson's poems among those of such traditional poets as Jean Chalmers Donaldson and Bess Foster Smith is, we think, both startling and appropriate. Formalist poetry written in conventional, schematically rhymed, accentual-syllabic meter continues to be written alongside experimental, open, and free-form poems, and prior to World War II no clear preference for the latter had been established.

When Irene Welch Grissom compiled poems for the Idaho section of *The North America Book of Verse* (New York: Henry Harrison, 1939), she wrote: "Idaho is a young and vigorous state and its people have been too busy developing the resources to become cynical or sophisticated." She found themes "set in plain and simple moulds" and reflecting "the elemental forces," and she offered poems written by "busy people": "These writers of verse do not hope to startle a waiting world with the splendor of their imaginations."

These observations are largely valid, with exceptions like those of Ezra Pound, Forrest Anderson, and Norman Macleod standing out as "proving the rule." But we were struck fairly often by lines and images from poets whose lives *were* apparently mundane, busy and unsophisticated. Consider, for example, Ruth Bernice Mead's comment on the "dreary monotone" of the desert mountains:

I know you have no words for me tonight;
Only this perfect mountain weariness,
Supine before the luxury of fire.

Often throughout the poems in this section the writers have struck it rich, or perhaps they have been stricken. The poet Randall Jarrell reminds us that "A good poet is someone who manages, in a lifetime of standing in thunderstorms, to be struck by lightning five or six times." And Robert Frost notes that although the poem "assumes direction with the first line laid down," it also "runs a course of lucky events" before it ends in "a momentary stay against confusion."

Poets of a New State
(1900–1940)

VARDIS FISHER (1895–1968)/RIRIE

Dick Rowe

He might now be a poet, did he live
Where poetry's not transmuted into prose
By life's andantes and adagios
That exorcise the swift and fugitive.
He might have spurned what etiquettes connive
To keep a man respectable: the clothes
And attitudes of virtuous repose
He might have sloughed and managed to survive.

But no bright cunning and no searching wit
Were to keep his scruples lean and thinned.
As when a plant has bent before a wind,
Has broken and has gone its way with it:
So like a tumbleweed was he, intent
on easy ways: he found them, and he went.

Hank Radder

When he abjured religion and then cursed
The ones who taught it to him as a child,
Folks said such crazy doubt was not the first
By which bewildered souls had been beguiled.
Said one, "He'd be a Judas, if he durst,"
And said another, "He's just runnun wild
From too much thinkun"; and they watched and smiled,
And said, "Of evils, thinkun is the worst."

But all smiles faded as Hank grew serene
And settled down, without his god, to peace;
And those who kept their god could not release
The torment of their faith in him, or screen
From pious feet a disappearing doubt
Of crazy ways that let a demon out.

Joe Hunter

Time built a pioneer and set him down
Upon the grayest waste of Idaho.
He clubbed the desert and he made it grow
In broad and undulating fields of brown.
He laid his might upon it, stripped its frown
Of drought and thistles; till by sweat and glow
He left the aged and barren hills aglow
With color—and its flame was his renown.

Few loved him, many feared, and some would smirk
Derisively, and call his mind untaught;
Of foul speech, and unclean from head to feet,
Who poured his great dream into golden wheat;
Until his gnarled and calloused hands had wrought
A deep and quiet holiness of work.

DONALD BURNIE [DWIGHT LEEPER] (1891–1932)/LEWISTON

Eva Kelly

For centuries the great sun wheeled by
And high hung stars looked down at night,
Mute witness to the age-old mysteries
Of birth and death among the red men.
But when, on that dim morning long ago
My mother's trembling body flung me forth,
It was one of those events
On which whole histories are hung,
For I was the first white child
Born in Tsceminicum.
Rude, bearded men looked at me
In awed delight
As I lay mewing my sorrows
To the white breasts of my mother;
Chieftains of the tribe
Brought tribute from mountain and river;
And red old squaws looked at me knowingly
And at my mother, bound to us
In the great sisterhood of suffering.

Harry Gale

The chill of an ancient ice field
Was in my heart;
I feared neither man nor devil,
Nor woman, who is more dangerous than either.
I lived with one of Anita's women,
A come-on girl in the *Nicaragua*,
And once I cut the heart out of a man
Who tried to take her from me;
Cut his heart out and holding it
On the point of my dagger
Showed it to my woman,
Who fell in a faint
Among the spittoons in the sawdust.

Wild Moll

Stabbed to my molten heart
With the long, keen dagger of life,
I danced in the lean, blue flames
Of the passionate bonfires of the Frontier
To the applause of barbaric, epic men,
Twisting the poniard and tasting
Of the delicious pain of living.
Even now, in my conventional old age
The dagger still lies hid
Beneath the folds of my stiff, black dress.
Oh lean, blue flames,
Oh Life, stab me again!

EZRA POUND (1885–1972)/HAILEY

Moeurs Contemporaines
(Contemporary Manners)

I

Mr, Styrax   1

Mr. Hecatomb Styrax, the owner of
        a large estate
                and of large muscles,

A "blue" and a climber of mountains, has married
        at the age of 28,
He being at that age a virgin,
The term "virgo" being made male in mediaeval
    latinity;
        His ineptitudes
Have driven his wife from one religious excess to
        another.
She has abandoned the vicar
For he was lacking in vehemence;
She is now the high priestess
Of a modern and ethical cult,
        And even now Mr. Styrax
        Does not believe in aesthetics.

        2

His brother has taken to gipsies,
But the son-in-law of Mr. H. Styrax
Objects to perfumed cigarettes.
        In the parlance of Niccolo Machiavelli:
        "Thus things proceed in their circle";
        And thus the empire is maintained.

    II

Clara

At sixteen she was a potential celebrity
With a distaste for caresses.
She now writes to me from a convent;
Her life is obscure and troubled;
Her second husband will not divorce her;
Her mind is, as ever, uncultivated,
And no issue presents itself.
She does not desire her children,
Or any more children.
Her ambition is vague and indefinite,
She will neither stay in, nor come out.

    III

Soiree

Upon learning that the mother wrote verses,
And that the father wrote verses,

And that the youngest son was in a publisher's office,
And that the friend of the second daughter was
            undergoing a novel,
The young American pilgrim
Exclaimed:
          "This is a darn'd clever bunch!"

IV

Sketch 48 b. 11

At the age of 27
Its home mail is still opened by its maternal
      parent
And its office mail may be opened by
      its parent of the opposite gender.
It is an officer,
            and a gentleman,
                        and an architect.

V

"Nodier raconte . . ."

1

At a friend of my wife's there is a photograph,
A faded, pale brownish photograph,
Of the times when the sleeves were large,
Silk, stiff and large above the *lacertus*,
That is, the upper arm,
And decollete. . . .
                It is a lady,
She sits at a harp,
Playing,

And by her left foot, in a basket,
Is an infant, aged about 14 months,
The infant beams at the parent,
The parent re-beams at its offspring.
The basket is lined with satin,
There is a satin-like bow on the harp.

2

And in the home of the novelist
There is a satin-like bow on an harp.
You enter and pass hall after hall,
Conservatory follows conservatory,
Lilies lift their white symbolical cups,
Whence their symbolical pollen has been excerpted,
Near them I noticed an harp
And the blue satin ribbon,
And the copy of "Hatha Yoga"
And the neat piles of unopened, unopening books,

And she spoke to me of the monarch,
And of the purity of her soul.

VI

Stele

After years of continence
    he hurled himself into a sea of six women.
Now, quenched as the brand of Meleagar,
    he lies by the poluphloisboious sea-coast.

SISTE VIATOR.

VII

I Vecchii

They will come no more,
The old men with beautiful manners.

Il etait comme un tout petit garcon
With his blouse full of apples
And sticking out all the way round;
Blagueur! "Con gli occhi onesti e tardi,"

And he said:
        "Oh! Abelard!" as if the topic
Were much too abstruse for his comprehension,
And he talked about "the Great Mary,"

And said: "Mr. Pound is shocked at my levity."
When it turned out he meant Mrs. Ward.

And the other was rather like my bust by Gaudier,
Or like a real Texas colonel,
He said: "Why flay dead horses?
"There was once a man called Voltaire."

And he said they used to cheer Verdi,
In Rome, after the opera,
And the guards couldn't stop them,

And that was an anagram for Vittorio
Emanuele *Re D' Italia*,
And the guards couldn't stop them.

Old men with beautiful manners,
Sitting in the Row of a morning;
Walking on the Chelsea Embankment.

VIII

Ritratto

And she sad:
    "You remember Mr. Lowell,
"He was your ambassador here?"
And I said: "That was before I arrived."
And she said:
    "He stomped into my bedroom. . . .
(By that time she had got on to Browning.)
". . . stomped into my bedroom. . . .
"And said: 'Do I,
"'I ask you, Do I
"'Care too much for society dinners?'
"And I wouldn't say that he didn't.
"Shelley used to live in this house."

She was a very old lady,
I never saw her again.

ANNIE PIKE GREENWOOD (? -1958)/HAZLETON

The Farmer's Wife and Her Poem

When I was young I used to write, and so I will again . . .
but I must start the fire, at once, for dinner for the men.
I'll write about last night: the clouds were billowing up the
    sky . . .
I cannot get the oven hot enough to bake this pie!
The moon was like a wistful bride, so tender and so true
    . . .
These biscuits will be just the thing to serve with chicken
    stew.
As through an aisle of clouds she went, her veil a floating
    mist . . .
Barbed wire, Joe! Don't cry, my boy, I'll iodine your
    wrist.

Where was I? . . . When I wash these towels and mix a
    batch of dough,
and wash the dinner dishes, sweep, mop, and when I sew
these sugar sacks into a dress, and make that shirt for Joe,
and iron these clothes, and make some jam, and help the
    men to mow . . .
and when I've staked tomato plants so that the wind can't
    blow
them over . . . then, if it isn't time to cook again, I'll go
and write that poem!

As I Wear a Gown

For I must wear my love for you
as I wear a gown,
all delicate and glistening,
to dances in the town.
And I must laugh and dance in it,
and at the deep of night,
I'll take my lovely gown off
and hang it out of sight.
And I must not shed any tears,

nor feel a pang again,
though I must wear my lovely gown
to dance with other men.

Definition of Love

> Love is the unseen generation
> demanding to be born.
>   Schopenhauer

I am the generation that must come!
Heralded by no trumpet and no gun,
column by column I am marching in,
to fill the ranks left bare by death or sin.

I am the generation that must come!
I must come, and no man may stem my way.
Woman or man who did not give me life,
them I condemn to blood drained dry by tears . . .
cold desolation do I give to them,
the empty hearthstone and the desert years,
the body wasted and the soul's decay . . .
I care not what they be, I must have life!

I am the generation that must come!
I make the man to search the woman out;
I make the woman listen for the man;
I make them yearn to be one name, one flesh;
I make them quiver at the tender kiss . . .
they call it *love* . . . 'tis I who weave the mesh.
He who dares falter, falls beneath my ban . . .
I must have life, in spite of fears and doubt.

I am the generation that must come!
I make the woman die without the man;
I make the man go mad without his mate;
I make them both outrun the sweeping sun,
and write their names in yearning with the stars.
I am the call for life; I am the fate;
I am the cause since first the race began.

I am the generation that must come!
I must have life! And so I push and crowd
and call and plead and kill and glorify!
There must be new men ere the old men die . . .
the plan of God can wear no funeral shroud.

I am the generation that must come!
Heralded by no trumpet and no drum,
column by column I am marching in,
to fill the ranks left bare by death and sin.

IRENE WELCH GRISSOM (1873– ?)/IDAHO FALLS

Clearing Sagebrush

It stood alone, the crude low shack,
Tarred-paper walls, a blot of black
Against a vast and tawny plain
Men called "The Place of Little Rain."
The dusk was shot with crimson glow
From piles of sagebrush burning low,
The man who watched with eager gaze
The flaming sparks and purple haze,
Had torn and twisted all day long
Resisting fibers, tough and strong,
To rake in windrows, where the light
Made golden serpents in the night.

He did not see the arid land
Of drifting dust and desert sand,
The scanty grass and prickly-pear
That fought to hold a footing there.
He caught the flashing silver gleam
Of ripples dancing on a stream,
Now gayly winding all about
Through fields of green, then in and out
Of nodding grain, and everywhere
The water went the earth was fair
With growing things—the embers died—
The silent plain was dark and wide.

JANET ELLEN MILLER (?)/SANDPOINT

The Big Boss

He rides the hills in his hell-bent Ford
    Like a cowboy rides his cayuse;
At dawn he's away up on Trestle Creek,
    And the night still finds him loose
A-hittin' the trail to camp sixteen,
    Or dodgin' the white pine's fall.
He's anyplace—everyplace; no one knows;
    So you've got to "hit the ball."

The "Jacks" all grin when they see him come;
    "Vell, de big boss, he ban har";
But they bend their backs to the mighty strokes
    And the cut of the ax rings far.
He's small in size but a fearless eye
    Can read you through and through—
And it's "Good-by, Bo!" to the fellow who shirks
    When the boss sees something to do.

One time when the wood was just all aflame
    And the crew in a closed ravine
With a wind a-headin' right straight their way
    (The prettiest trap I've seen)
The "Big Boss" jumps in his trusty Ford,
    (Our cries of fear a-scornin'—)
And he rode back singed like an old black cat—
    But he'd saved the men by his warnin'.

Now the lumberjacks from the camps all around
    When they meet in a nearby town,
Tell tales of the "Big Boss" and his ways
    When he, in his Ford, drops down!
But all of them know in their own deep souls,
    When for help they're at a loss,
That the one they turn to (in thick or thin)
    Is the much-abused "Big Boss."

PAUL CROY (1905–)/WORLEY

The Riverpig

The work of the day is begun for the Jacks
And they greet it with eager hands,
With ribald quip from a bulging lip,
These sons of the rough hard land.
The Push is in front and he swings along,
And the crew files out behind,
For life is good in the morning wood
And they sneer at a crabbed mind.

Their joints are stiff and their muscles sore,
And it's cold in the early fog,
But the mists will lift when the sunrays sift
Down to the river bog.

They reach the rear before the sun
Has melted the ice-scummed sloughs,
And the day is done ere the wage is won
That they'll spend on women and booze.

It's dangerous work on the Center and Wings,
But they laugh as they cuff the logs;
A-slip, is a man on a racing jam
But it's crossed at an easy jog.
If a Jack slips into an eddy's whirl
From a buckskin's slimy bark,
They laughingly jeer and they lift him clear
And they treat the thing as a lark.

It's a hardy life for roughened men
But they scoff at its many scars,
As they trip the wings where the current swings
And sack them off o' the bars.

When the season's spree of a Jack is done,
Of the big spring drive he'll think,
Where the rushing sweep of the soup is deep
You can stand up here and drink.

For the perfect dream of a Riverpig
Is a river smooth and flat,
Where a log will ride like a ship at tide,
And a man can float his hat.
And they love their work as a sailor his,
And they come back year by year
To answer the call where the big jams haul,
As the spring flats lure the deer.

For it is a work they love and know
That none can do so well
As a Riverpig, with his snoose and swig
And a hearty scorn for hell.

RUTH BERNICE MEAD (1895– ?)/CALDWELL

Mountain Interlude

(A Woman Speaks)

You have gone far upon the hills today,
The blue of distances is in your eyes,
The stillness of old dreams upon your face.
Out where the rhythm of the endless hills,
So much alike, so wearisomely steep,
The dreary monotone of gray-brown ranks
Breaks in an even surge against the sky,
You lay, all spent, upon a sun-hot rock;
The broken rhythm of your heart flung up
Its challenge to the meaning of the sky.

I know you have no words for me tonight;
Only this perfect mountain weariness,
Supine before the luxury of fire.
I move my rose vase from the mantel lest
Their softness blur the pungent cedar scent;
Tomorrow's round will bring us words enough,
Let me but help to keep untouched tonight
The misty blue of distance in your eyes,
The stillness of old dreams upon your face.

KEITH BARRETTE (?)/BLACKFOOT

Rural Etching

A flock of crows circles in a sky of slate,
A lazy wind loafs in the willows,
In the damp black field a team of bays
The plowman follows; fresh furrows run
Back and forth in staggering monotony.

Supper fire smoke curls upward,
Sways for a moment like a willow tip
Then merges into the immensity of space.
Children scream at their evening play
Throwing handsful of dust into the air,
Watching it burst into straggling clouds.
A flivver rattles by, scattering the peace
Of the countryside into jets of chaotic
Realism.

Then night throws a sack enveloping the remaining day
The concrete world merges and blends into shadows,
Leaving nothing definite, nothing real.
The crows have gone, the wind is still,
The empty field silent, throwing its long furrows
Completely into the pit of obscurity.
And through a cottage window shines a lamp light,
A feeble effort against the strong inevitable
Power of night.

YVOR WINTERS (1900–1968)/MOSCOW

Nocturne

Moonlight on stubbleshining hills
whirls down upon me finer than geometry
and at my very
face it blurs and softens like a dream

In leafblack houses
linen smooth with sleep
and folded by cold life itself for limbs so definite

their passion is
persistent like a pane of glass

about their feet the clustered
birds are sleeping
heavy with incessant life

The dogs swim close to earth

A killdee rises
dazed and rolled amid the sudden blur of sleep
above the dayglare of the fields
goes screaming
off toward darker hills

The Journey

(Snake River Country)

I now remembered slowly how I came,
I, sometime living, sometime with a name,
Creeping by iron ways across the bare
Wastes of Wyoming, turning in despair,
Changing and turning, till the fall of night,
Then throbbing motionless with iron might.
Four days and nights! Small stations by the way,
Sunk far past midnight! Nothing one can say
Names the compassion they stir in the heart.
Obscure men shift and cry, and we depart.

And I remembered with the early sun
That foul-mouthed barber back in Pendleton,
The sprawling streets, the icy station bench,
The Round-up pennants, the latrinal stench.
These towns are cold by day, the flesh of vice
Raw and decisive, and the will precise;
At night the turbulence of drink and mud,
Blue glare of gas, the dances dripping blood,
Fists thudding murder in the shadowy air,
Exhausted whores, sunk to a changeless stare.
Alive in empty fact alone, extreme,
They make each fact a mortuary dream.

Once when the train paused in an empty place,
I met the unmoved landscape face to face;
Smoothing abysses that no stream could slake,
Deep in its black gulch crept the heavy Snake,
The sound diffused, and so intently firm,
It seemed the silence, having change nor term.
Beyond the river, gray volcanic stone
In rolling hills: the river moved alone.
And when we started, charged with mass, and slow,
We hung against it in an awful flow.

Thus I proceeded until early night,
And, when I read the station's name aright,
Descended—at the building of a word!
I slept the night out where the thought occurred,
Then rose to view the dwelling where I lay.
Outside, the bare land stretching far away;
The frame house, new, fortuitous, and bright,
Pointing the presence of the morning light;
A train's far screaming, clean as shining steel
Planing the distance for the gliding heel.
Through shrinking frost, autumnal grass uncurled,
In naked sunlight, on a naked world.

CAROL RYRIE BRINK (1895–1980) /MOSCOW

The Fairy Wife

She was all red and gold—
A laughing creature.
We farm lads left the fold,
Running to reach her.

All the lads fell far behind,
Only I caught her.
(How my old mother pined
With her for daughter!)

She was so sweet and young,
Like a straight willow.
Golden her long hair hung
Over my pillow.

Sometimes she sang at first,
Skimming my cream;

Scouring my hearth it burst—
Music like dream.

Sometimes her feet would dance
Ere winter froze her;
Then must I pause to glance,
Glad that I chose her.

But with the early dawn
And the long waking,
All her wild whims have gone,
Her beauty taking.

I might have picked a score,
Thicker and stronger,
Who would have labored more
And lasted longer.

Foggy Day at the Beach

The breakers come rolling in out of the fog;
From nothing, all this fuss and foam
That boils and thunders at my feet,
Like dark green glass exploding
Into a profusion of white flowers.
Out of nowhere, out of nowhere
Come the passionate waves
To break and dissipate upon the sands.

Thoughts on Eating an Apple

When I cut the green globe of the apple,
A snug worm was revealed.
He had made a clever house for himself
With rooms and passages,
All neat and tidy, very much alone.
He was eating his way out
With patient appetite.

He never foresaw me, the lordly giant
Who bought him at the supermarket.
He felt himself a king,
Master of a self-sufficient universe,
But there are kings beyond kings,
Giants beyond giants,
Gods beyond gods,
And beyond the green globe of our little earth,
Planets beyond planets.

JEAN CHALMERS DONALDSON (1885–1972)/MOSCOW

Back Street Autumn

Busy all the day among her jars and kettles
With crimson berry-jam and toothsome plum,
She does not realize the roses' petals
Are weeping that, at last, their hour has come.
She has no time to watch a slumberous flower
Fold up its petals in a neat array,
Not realizing that this languid hour
Foretold the coming of its final day.
She has not seen the seeded hillsides vary
From green to golden coverlets where light
And shadow play; it is hers to be wary
Lest winter come; thus she must set her might
Against an empty larder. . . . John, he drinks;
She is a fine provider—so he thinks.

Young Farm Wife

The rain is pelting the window
With little tacks;
Out in the pasture the cattle
Are humping their backs.

The sky is a dripping curtain
Folding about the day
And it seems to her that the sunshine
Is gone to stay.

A click of the gate and a dog's bark—
She hears as an undertone—
Like a flash she forgets she was ever
There in the rain alone.

Hollyhocks

I have seen bougainvillia on a wall,
Vivid and glowing in the southern sun,
And I have tip-toed past them lest there fall
A footstep that might leave their spell undone—
And poinsettias—their scarlet bracts
Have charmed me into sudden breathlessness
With sheer splendor—I have seen gay tracts
Of tulips preening, each in Sunday dress.

And once I came upon a perfect garden
With rosetrees slender as a marshland reed
Abloom and fragrant. Need I ask your pardon
If I should say that all of these, indeed,
Have given me not half the happy sense
Of hollyhocks along my own back fence?

Velvet Foil

There is no word more beautiful than hush—
A muted symphony for tired ears;
It is the hope of little winds that rush
Homeward before their rival, night, appears.
It is the haze caressing amber hills
When evening closes fast her final door;
It is the spirit of the trees; the trills
Of sleepy linnets in the sycamore.

And when my foolish feet, at times, must stray
Into the clang and clatter of the street,
It comes to whisper in my ear and say,
"Out there the sound of everything is sweet . . ."
Then to my woodland place I turn and rush
To wrap myself in velvet foil of hush.

FORREST ANDERSON (1903– ?)/WEISER

springboard as a waterfront cafe

abor
charges his undershot fist closes
around the flask and lean zinc proclivities
and lean one pipe one fume
one is ashamed in a safe room

the goad
reactivated there for
a thousandth first-time he
showed his back to destinations

what could
i forbid beneath a found ledge
where the treasure, partner.
this pearl
tears my eye, and i
have lost the right to desire

more than the ocean mute beats
let us be for five minutes mad
let us be mute
despite the salty algebra in your grin, our boat
is dry our anchor is behind and the sea
like a disastrous flower
opens to receive us.

definitions

this love and all loves and love simply
word in whose shadow i have ever leaned
who am in the shade of him i must one day be
or never be but as these i see as none is seen

against which code your music beats, drops
tick and harmony, roll and repeat on whom it
lets fall a most insistent code. love needs
no code other than its own, with me, near me

so sharply sings what my feelings think
of lips and hands denied to love, of love
the hands and feet would not have taken
you on voyages away from what you seek

o love, deliver us from love, please
tell the head of the heart to speak
its codes as far as music. love's longest
voyages will find your truth at my heart's feet.

vol fantasque

comets are drunk, stars caught in the green
bottle of friendship so change may come
that the self should find its sun the being
might rocket up the slope of air to some other
light the leak of what is solid in it are
hazard and i flying on an audaciously
                                    frail mechanics
as unrealities rise i almost reach my real
lack of any wish except to travel to
nowhere and back again a sailor for your sea of
red excess, a slow pedestrian across your body's
                                              forests
                                              almost
an aviator against your symmetric breath, but
nothing sends me soon to everything since
the only voyages are alone.
go we, then, alone and all fast into
the place of what a love could mean without a birth in beauty, his death in truth.

BESS FOSTER SMITH (1887– ?)/WEISER

Country Store

Some ways I'm like a country store:
    My mind gets in a clutter;
My sentiments keep running o'er
    Like tubs of melting butter.

My thoughts, still in the embryo,
   Resemble the stale eggs;
My memories, dried herring so
   Long packed away in kegs.

My dispositioned vinegar,
   My rather strong-willed cheese
(Opinionated Limburger),
   Float out upon the breeze.

I do have sweet molasses jugs,
   Some spice and peppermint,
Some soothing Old Gold twist or plug,
   Bright calico and print.

So I am like a country store,
   With bits of this and that;
Most anything you're looking for,
   And no aristocrat!

But just an unpretentious place
   As any country store may be;
And I pray I never lack its grace
   Of cordiality.

Norman Macleod (1906–1985)/Weiser

Evening Above the Snake

At Weiser our sweaters were a sunset for the evening
As we leaned against the railings of the bridge
Over the Snake River. The park on the island
Was a wanness of electric lights, and the bushes
Were a distillation of love. We were tired
Of shooting bee-bee guns and were too young to drink.
We smoked cigarettes as a gesture of manhood
And bolstered the breast with our breath,
Proud of our prowess in athletics. It must have been risky
To pass the blaze of our sweaters at dark.

Ring Around the Syringas: 1920

Along the Clark Fork of the Columbia
The shooting stars were out of purple ground, rock-
Sharpened rain-teeth in the sky:
A man may have died in Hellgate canyon but the odor
Of his brandy breath remains, mackinaw-
Frosted in rabbit weather.

Aunt Crystal, who
Of all my aunts was the favorite—
Who raised radishes and planted pears
With equal relish
On her ranch in the mountains
And who, alone of the rest, rode
With her heel-heft in the iron hide:
The mare's flat ear pointed—
Until

My Uncle Will came along—
A fine friend when the forest would let him—
But hot for the Ku Klux Klan
And that was why
My Uncle Morgan
Was angry, his alfalfa going to seed
And Debs on the gramaphone and his wife, my Aunt
Candace, wild with worry

And his son, Aubrey,
A queer duck doctoring his warts
With milkweed, packing his prospector's kit
Into the jasper mountains (the spitting
Image of his father: could spit
Tobacco juice like a grasshopper).

But when Uncle Morgan slapped down
Uncle Will for riding around
In bedsheets with the K.K.K.—
The summer sour in his belly—
Father and son set out for gold in the mountains

And Uncle Will
Retreated to Crystal's ranch,

Where Glenette (his last born) under the rocker
Was uttering her first-born cries: and all of us
Cluttering the kitchen
With our eyes.

And Crystal heard
How
Uncle Will
Would be a forest ranger
Come next week and never
Speak to anyone again, the chipmunks
Calling him, and his wounded pride
A band-aid to protect his hate.

But
The radishes, peaches, the potatoes:
Embarrassed strawberries even—
Anyhow, it would soon be snow,
The frost of late September on the sun
And rusty carrots nailed into the bin,

For a man
Has served his marriage well,
Come children to the woodshed, their blistered
Behinds—

But Uncle Morgan was lost
To Candace, Debs and socialism,
Digging for gold in the mountains . . .

While along the Bitterroots
The ducks were out and soon it would be
Venison weather.

I buttoned
My stag-
Shirt
Over my heart.

EDNA GILLESPIE (?)/?

Wall-Flower

To you who like slender lances,
Sway your way through the dances.
We who sit along the wall,
Dull and quiet as an old gray shawl,
Seem but futile and absurd,
As you flash by with careless word;
We turn and nod with frozen grin
And bitter prayer deep within
That the gods may smite and grind
All that beauty to powder, and bind
A starry atom to our head
That we may sparkle among the dead.

E. A. BRUBACHER (?)/?

Joe Weaver of Owyhee

I am Joe Weaver, the trapper.
    I'm old but I'll push up the trail
In spite of the wrath of the blizzard—
    Nothing yet made me fail.

Hugging the cliffs of the mountains,
    Running my trap line out there,
Knowing the chill of the wind's clip,
    Feeling the frost's cold air.

Knowing the trail of the coyote—
    That slinking and tawny one,
Laying my traps for the cougar,
    Giving the fates a run.

Giving the fates a run, boys,
    Playing the cards that I draw—
Holding the high cards sometimes,
    And sometimes stuck on the raw.

I've sinned lots of sins, I know it,
   As down life's way I've trod,
But I know that the birds in the bushes
   Are singing for love of God.

I've drunk red whiskey and liked it—
   Warming me up inside;
I've gone on a bust—Oh brother!
   Rolling both high and wide.

I've thrown my money around some
   In the cow-town down the line,
I've taken my fling at the tables
   Making my dollars whine.

I've followed the trail of the red stars
   When the desert was empty,
I've builded my lonely campfire
   And dreamed alone in the night.

I'll find my place in the finish,
   Of Simon called Peter, I've read,
And someone, perhaps, will remember
   To speak up for "Joe" when he's dead.

AMY WOODWARD FISHER (1889– ?)/MOSCOW

Rain in Harvest

The August rain fell slowly, steadily.
It washed the dust from the picket fence;
It fell on the combine in the pea field.
The zinnias and pansies smiled and sparkled
Like the faces of freshly rubbed children ready for a party.
The trees were quiet and peaceful
As church people waiting their turn at sentence prayers.
The farmer and his wife bowed their heads at the breakfast
    table.
She smiled
And blessed the rain for the good that it would do.
He did not smile.
He was quiet like the red fir trees in the yard;

His eyes glittered as the pearls of rain
That clung to their drooping branches.

EDITH M. ROBERTS (?)/?

Idaho Potato Field

Two wee lads in a dark brown field
among the sacks;
lifting their pails with cold blue hands
and tired backs.

The last one emptied, they wait for Dad,—
(this field is done);
they drag about, too cold to rest,
too tired for fun.

The father comes and shrewdly scans
the naked row;
no hint of plan, no word of praise
does he bestow.

We watch them follow down the road
with troubled mind
(The littlest one looks so forlorn,
trailing behind).

Will life bring aught of golden grain
and fruit to till?
Or endless rows of tuber sacks
in brown, to fill?

The Third Generation
❦ *(1940–1980)*

Introduction

ACCORDING TO THE *IDAHO BLUE BOOK*, IDAHO'S POPULATION doubled every ten years between 1870 (nearly 15,000) and 1910 (325,594), then grew by 100,000 or less every decade through 1970, increasing by only about 14,000 between 1920 and 1930. Between 1970 and 1980, however, the population soared by over 200,000 (to 944,127). In compiling the poems of the "third generation," we found a commensurate increase in the number of poets whose work might be said to "represent" the state, many of them coming into print in the 1970s, so this section of the anthology proved challenging with respect to the volume of material to be surveyed. As always, the hardest task was that of making value judgments, which requires that editors keep their sword blades broad at the same time that they keep them finely honed.

The population of Idaho has become increasingly urban. The 1970 census marks the point at which more than half the population could be classified as "urban," and although Idaho may always remain more "rural" in nature than most states of the union, and although "urban" in Idaho appears to mean something very different from "urban" in California, that year clearly marks a period of important literary development. It was in the mid-1970s, for example, that Ahsahta Press at Boise State University began publishing its poetry series with *The Selected Poems of Norman Macleod* and Confluence Press at Lewis-Clark State College began the literary magazine, *Slackwater Review*, and its series of chapbooks and magazines. The anthology which Ron McFarland edited in 1979, *Eight Idaho Poets* (University of Idaho Press), also reflects that cultural boom, which was nourished by the National Endowments for the Arts and the Humanities and the Poets-In-The-Schools program via state agencies (Idaho Commission on the Arts, Idaho Humanities Commission) and by the state's colleges and universities.

The population of Idaho, like that of all other states in this nation, has also become increasingly mobile in the years following World War II. More than any other section of the anthology, this one reflects the editors' awareness of the flow of population, which makes it virtually impossible to account for the characteristics of a "real" Idaho poet. Some of the poets here, like Vern Rutsala and Richard Shelton, are Idaho natives who left the state during their childhood, but whose work has drawn on their early experiences. Other poets, like Ed Dorn and Kim Stafford, resided in the state only a few years. But all of the poets included here have reflected Idaho in their work, and we believe they have a legitimate place in this anthology. We have not included, on the other hand, the many renowned poets who have visited college campuses for residencies of various durations, from a few days to a full semester, even though many of them have recorded their discovery of Idaho in their work.

Stylistically, this section shows considerable variety. From the sonnet by Idaho's second poet laureate, Sudie Stuart Hager of Kimberly, named by Governor C. A. Robbins in 1949, to Vern Rutsala's sestina and Kim Stafford's villanelle, the traditional "fixed forms" are amply represented. But free or open form in poetry has predominated in Idaho as it has throughout the country, particularly since World War II. We have also remained receptive to a variety of voices, ranging from Bonnie Cochrane Hirsch's delightfully comic "Me an Mason Williams Down the Garden Path" to Richard Shelton's 90-line historical poem, "Harry Orchard," which reflects upon the prison life of the man who assassinated ex-governor Frank Steunenberg in 1905.

Many of the poets whose work appears in this section are still living and writing, but because they have left the state, we chose to place their poems here, along with the those of poets now deceased whose work appeared between 1940 and 1980. The poems are printed in alphabetical order by the poets' names, from Duane Ackerson to Charles David Wright, and we have included parenthetically their city or town of residence.

The Third Generation (1940–1980)

DUANE ACKERSON/POCATELLO

Beforehand

Each finger on the hand
has its own story to tell
but the thumb, the body's accomplice,
pushes them into line
and this poem gets written.

The paper would like to return to the tree
or even lie in a pile of rags on some floor,
without a word to say
or the nobility of a watermark,
but opacity meters report
that it is just the right thickness,
and it goes in the package,
and this poem gets written.

The typewriter would like to think its own thoughts,
forming words slowly, quiet as a convention
of sleepy crickets, perhaps
even speaking its own language,
which has a silvery sound
that leaves a dark afterimage in the mind,
but someone has dragged it into a dark alley
and is beating the blood out of it
and this poem gets written

Weathering

You told us about chairs
made out of doors,
rough-hewn and left outside
so the joints could fill and grow
together in the rain.
These chairs could last fifty years
on the front porch, you said,
and fall apart
with a year of the parlor.

Watching you at dinner,
tan face, knotted arms,
your wife pale as fresh cut timber,
I could see you knew
what sort of carpentry
you were.

JAMES ATER/MURTAUGH

mountain vigil

the night horse picks a quiet way to stand
at the outer edge of light
the red dog starts
remarks the horse well known to him
then querulously turns back his head
onto my blanket end

now awake i half-arise
to toss a stick onto the fire
and check the skies

a pendant moon's low in my eye
and slowly venus peeks
up from the eastern edge of night
the hustle of a wanton breeze
dusts the ashes from the fire
and skirls away again

down off the ridge the coyote bitch
i ran off yesterday
starts talking to her cubs back home
telling them to stay
she's made her kill and coming in
with meat for this fine day

now light begins to loom the sky

the night has slipped away

JAMES BROCK/BOISE

The Growth of Mathematics

Every electric kernel of light
that shimmers from a falling wave
is held by an equation that assumes
all variables: gravity, wind,
inertia. If we stop everything,
the curve may be as pure and certain
as $y = \sin x$. But this is the white love
of self-evident axioms: somewhere
nearing the speed of light, all lines
converge out of necessity.

Today, my love, I have read twelve
love poems by my students,
so many little cartoons of a big heart
to contend with, so many refrigerators
two-thirds empty, windows
over oceans. Waves upon
waves. So what wave shall I proffer
you? Here I could point to our cats,
tame as love, watching a nuthatch
upside-down. I could offer
you an egg, warm and almost liquid with life
in your hand. I could give you something.

Walking to the university, I hold
your books, your arm rests like need
around my waist. Somewhere off Alaska,
my friend Tyler tries to forget
his aunt, the nuclear physicist, by chasing
salmon, the trawl lines slack. Somewhere
in Nebraska, two men younger than I
wait near a missile silo, their shift
beginning. If I could, I'd find
a truer arithmetic, or something
that would define the curve
of your arm, there, the presence,
the wave of your body.

The Recognition of Beasts

Beneath Lake Stanley, the kokanee run, red
extinction deep in olive water. Lodgepole
and ponderosa soldier the lake; what can hold
this together? Not the redfish, spent dead
in instinct, not the Sawtooths, this shiver
of granite, not forests, nor swallows,
nor us. What ordering we impose hollows
experience. To discover a river
from which we came and name it is the wrong
way to force love. Nothing's saved from what we
devise. Then remember the deer struck blind
by our lantern—the white-tailed doe and fawn
frozen, one body paralyzed—as we
recognize our paralysis, our one mind.

ED DORN/POCATELLO

Home on the Range, February, 1962

Flutes, and the harp on the plain
Is a distance, of pain, and waving reeds
The scale of far off trees, notes not of course
Upon a real harp but chords in the thick clouds
And the wind reaching its arms toward west yellowstone.
Moving to the east, the grass was high once, and before
White wagons moved
                              the hawk, proctor of the hills still is
Oh god did the chunky westerner think to remake this in
        his own image
Oh god did the pioneer society sanctify the responsible
        citizen
To do that
                    face like a plot of ground
Was it iron locomotives and shovels, hand tools
And barbed wire motives for each man's
Fenced off little promised land
                              or the mind of bent

Or of carson, oh earp
These sherpas of responsible destruction
Posses led by a promising girl wielding a baton upon the
    street
A Sacagawea wearing a baseball cap, eating a Clark bar.
And flutes and the harp are on the plain
Bring the last leading edge of stillness
Brought no water, brought dead roots
Like an allotment of tool handles to their premises—and
    they cry
In pain over daily income—a hundred years of planned
    greed
Loving the welfare state of new barns and bean drills
Hot passion for the freedom of the dentist!
Their plots were america's first subdivisions called
    homesteads

Lean american—gothic quarter sections gaunt look
Managing to send their empty headed son who is a ninny
to nebraska to do it, all over again, to the ground, a prairie
Dog hole,
And always they smirk at starvation
And consider it dirty . . . a joke their daughters learn
From their new husbands.

Chronicle

It is January 12
and midwinter, the great dipper
stands on its handle in the sky
over pocatello.
The air, a presence
around the body when I go out
the door to relieve myself
is well below zero.

Yes it is well below.
This land is well
below, say shoot it, longitude
and latitude, yet it stings
like the Yukon, and standing,
to get back to that,

I thumb my nose several times
at the city below, it is midnight
and the lights are stationary
through the cool absent fog.

Inside Fred plays his cello
and that air sings thereby.
I run my fingers through my hair.
Here, all around, is
the world, out
on points, on the horizon are
friends close and far gone.
With the tautness of those
chorded strings bind them
together,
this air will kill us all
ere long.

CAROLYN S. FOOTE/BOISE

Widow

Living alone
produces conditions
undreamed of before:

sudden ignitions
of strange appetite
for unsuitable food
and drink
late at night,
a penchant for letting
disorder pertain
in household and person,
a hearty disdain
for anything useful.

My mind's vacuum vacant;
if I didn't know better,
I'd think I was pregnant.

Reflections

inspired (partly) by
Judy's Screen Door

Times passionate and frustrate beyond sense
Are not the times I miss you most.

                        The hands
Once urgent towards the aching, sweet consent
Of joining flesh could also soothe demands
From dripping faucets, choke that sticks and stalls,
Patchy plaster falling off the walls
U-joints leaking, wires that spit and burn,
Solenoids gone scatty.

                        How I yearn
To lead you to the bedroom, where the lamp
Blinks screwloose in its socket, to the damp
Recesses downstairs where the furnace fire
Grows feeble, to the washer and the dryer,
Both sullen in their niches!

                        My desire
For kisses still distracts me, but your skills
Could smooth away a host of other ills!

SUDIE STUART HAGER/KIMBERLY

A Spider Web in a Rose Garden

This shimmering web is hung from flower to flower,
A perfect wheel of finest silken threads;
I saw the spider struggle, hour on hour,
To bind it firmly to the soft rose-heads.
He worked as if he meant this web to last
The summer through, catch many luscious flies;
He hid himself from insects travelling past,
And now is watching with contented eyes.

He soon will learn his labor was in vain,
For both the blooms are shattering in the sun;
Tomorrow he must build his web again,
And even then his task may not be done.

And, oh, my heart laments to see him fail;
Today I built my dream on things as frail!

KENNETH O. HANSON/SHELLEY

Montana

Just over the border
a handful of stores
both sides of the road—
grocery, filling station, feed store
drug store, depot, tavern.

I wait on the platform
for the one daily train south.
The vapors of summer rise over the rails
and the dust shines, north and south.
From somewhere a black dog
is going home obliquely.

After three months
I still don't much want to leave.
Every day like today—arid & flat & spare
but with beautiful small signs
as August dies.

Now there's a fat blues
spilling from the door of Ed's Happy Haven
and the neon comes on
(before night does)
seeming to say to me Don't
go Don't go Come back

JIM HEYNEN/BOISE

Traveling through Idaho on Opening Day

From Coeur d'Alene
down 95, the quiet lake
like an arm
next to my arm, resting.

We will tell no one
of this, this silent,
this air, this cool
breath of cedar.
We whisper the naming
of parts—"noble fir,
hemlock, blue spruce."

Everywhere the green trees
sway, the grass,
the wind, a congregation
of solitude. We
will tell no one of this.

Nor of the sudden
elk stumbling
from shadows now
on the road
bewildered by light.

We will tell no one,
nor listen to his
rumor of blood
following from trees,
nor of the laughter,
the first drum-beats of morning.

Sioux Center, Iowa

Home of the Christian smile.
Not a center for Sioux.
The Dutch. A sub-
culture of yah's. Calvin-
istic and clean. Deep

winters. Sustained
by corn and thick
holsteins, creamy
grins, and providencial
care. Straight
furrows surround
the town. No mote,
no dike to protect it.
Only the creamery and grain
elevator, the old hatchery,
truck stops,
and many bristling
steeples.

Do you think the people are nice?
The people are not nice.
The people are right.
Do you think the people are clean?
The people are clean.

Mosquitoes and white lawn chairs.
Ping pong in the basement.
Pictures of horses.
Miniature German Shepherds
in back car windows, their eyes
blinking the turns.
Pictures of lonely hands
praying.

Do you think the people like baseball?
The people like baseball.
Do you think the people love?
The people love what is right.

John Deere and snowmobiles
and predestination for those
whom it hurts. Polished saddles.
Salads with whipped cream
and marshmallows. Thick
steaks.

Do you think the young people
drive in circles with new cars?

The young people
drive in circles with new cars.
The young people drive in circles
with new cars until they are aroused.
The new cars stop near cornfields
and graveyards and rock
in their tracks.

Do you think the people know the Beautiful?
A daughter in a white gown
who can play the church organ.
Do you think the people drink whiskey?
The people drink whiskey
in the next county.
Do you think the people would like you?
The people would not like you. You
are not one of them. But you
are important
where you are. God
loves everyone
who stays in his place.

BONNIE COCHRANE HIRSCH/BOISE

Knighthood in Grangeville

She should have been a rainbow-skirted dancer,
the one the king adores but cannot marry,
the dark-eyed one with secret healing powers,
whose dance before the villain saves the kingdom.

She wasn't meant to spend her life in Grangeville,
bound in such a solemn heavy body,
but he paused while counting up his nickels
and assumed the shining crown she offered him.

He said she was the Beauty of the Kingdom.
Her sagging shoulders said that she denied it.
He shrugged his, turned back to his canned goods;
she sighed, and starched and ironed his shirts.

He labored on, selling beans and cabbage,
and spent his evenings tracing family roots
searching for a drop of royal blood
to break the spell and let her whirl away.

Me an Mason Williams,
Down the Garden Path

How bout them zucchini growers,
aint they good?
Sneakin they old squash around the
neighborhood.
Always grow too many,
never pickem small.
Stuffem down the family
til they wants to bawl.
Watchem growin faster
than they hands can pick.
Servem every dinner
til they gittin sick.
Never pickem liddle,
lettem grow too big.
Feedem to the neighbors,
feedem to the pig.
How to grow zucchini?
Quickest thing around.
Gitcherself a buncha seeds,
shove em ina ground.

JIM IRONS/BOISE

Insomnia

I'll drink until the words disappear.
God doesn't love those who can't sleep.
Hell may be this night without a drink.
Hell may be having to live your life over.

There's a tranquilizer in the cabinet.
I'll save it until I need it.
The idea of poetry and sickness . . .
I find it so rebarbative.

The idea of it, the very idea . . .
I'd like to take sentiment and wring its neck!
Where is the woman I loved with real love?
Where is a woman when you need one?

The idea of poetry & sickness . . .
Be glad when you pass from the world of feeling.
Hell may be pain squared, pain cubed.
Hell may be complete repetition.

If I told you that hell may be what you are doing
    right now!
Doomed to repeat that moment endlessly . . .
You'd change your life!
Hell may be having to live your life over.

EDNA CASTER JOLL/BOISE

The Plumcot Tree

In the dark secrecy of earth
Roots seeking white blossoms.
Deeper and deeper searching
Feeling the fragrance, tracing the shape of the flower.
What does the earth give
To make five white petals?

      Heart that I love
      Break for me
      Earth's white gift to the plumcot tree.

In the blue mysteries of Heaven
Branches seeking white blossoms
Higher and higher reaching
Into the dawn sky, into the midnight splendors.
What does the sky give
To make five white petals?

      Heart that I love
      Touch tenderly
      Heaven's white gift to the plumcot tree.

Matthew

They thought old Matthew mad because he spoke
About the sky as though it were the earth.
He sowed and reaped his fields, but he declared
The sky held things that grew, beyond the worth
Of anything that land produced. He said
If man would learn the way to harvest space
His wants would all be satisfied. Folks grinned;
But Matthew's eyes shone quiet, like his face.

One night he climbed the barren, rocky knoll
By which one corner of his farm was bound.
The ones who saw him go there were the last
To see him: Matthew vanished, sight and sound.
Some say he wandered off in foot and mind.
Jim Collins' boy, age five, says Matt grew wings,
And that he saw him binding sheaves of stars.
. . . You know how children all imagine things.

GRACE EDGINGTON JORDAN/BOISE

Rest in Peace

"Nearly every ranch in the canyon has a grave, many
unmarked, many known only to the oldtimers."

Close to Low saddle the trail runs by
A cairn, unmarked except to the eye
That saw a boy not fourteen yet
On a crazy horse, in the dark and wet,
Determined to do a man's work or die.

Where the pear trees shower their wasted bloom,
Someone sleeps in the greenish gloom
Of the matted brush on a homestead claim;
Sleeps without crucifix, date or name.
Forgotten pear trees; forgotten tomb.

In a lordly half-moon river bend,
Warmed by sun and caressed by wind,
The marble stone that shields D.K.
Is often upset by a colt at play.

But that's no offense, since in a way
D.K.'s was rather a riotous end.

Temperance creek was days from rail,
Exit only by mule and trail;
Where better await Bill's recompense
With his name on a neat encircling fence,
Dimly hearing coyote and quail.

Some blood that smeared the canyon red
Was not for cards or women shed.
Twenty Chinese washing gold
Were watched from the rim and shot down cold.
God flay the guilty wherever they are,
And rest the Chinks on their haunted bar.

On many a creek an ashy square
With fringe of charred log tells you where
A cabin stood. But how it went
Sinisterly or by accident,
No hint the scorched trees bare.
A bone that resisted the licking flames,
Overalls buttons, glasses frames;
Knife and heel plates, all in a heap—
The burnt trees moan and your neck hairs creep.
Men do die along the Snake
But where fire's been, you'd better not rake.

Egg and Ode

A hen can lay an egg a day;
A daily ode no poet writes,
Yet still how like are egg and ode—
Elegant case round an interlude.
At least that's how they seem to be,
Crammed with substance and nice to see.

O hen, scorn not your slower rival;
True art is related to survival;
Spilt egg on vest may last a week,
But Eternity's what poets seek,
And how they bleed throughout invention.
But you, hen, feel just good intention.

GREG KEELER/POCATELLO

American Falls

At 4:00 a.m., I drove to American Falls
through twenty miles of southern Idaho
to where the Snake stopped between canyon walls
behind the dam then roared out below.

Over the foaming forebay on catwalks
old men had already established themselves,
eyes fixed on current-bent rods, backs
bent to the spray. And from the swells

they pulled flopping rainbows, huge balloons
of flesh. They used nightcrawlers, sucker-meat on
cheap hooks with lots of weight. I fished spoons
that only worked for a thin hour of dawn.

Between cement walls and the turbines, the fish
were ours or chopped up before the river
was itself again. And the old men, fresh
for death, knew this better than I, whether

or not they showed me their stringers.
No one had to mention humility under the
terrible sound of water getting thinner
with one place to go. When we'd see

Union Pacific scream over the top of the dam,
it was only a whisper to us, like the lines
in our fingers, whistling a secret hymn
deep into the howl, searching for signs

of present-tense rainbows. The smoke
of a phosphate plant rose with dead fish
above the banks, always out to tell us no
and keep us trying, flicking our wrists

toward flux. Now it's all framed. They're dead.
Their clusters of fat trout swam out of time.
A smooth new dam is there instead—
no forebay, just water in a hard, thin line.

ROSEMARY KLEIN/MOSCOW

Last Words

Almost off the couch, you are falling
through the frame of your photograph, your smile turned
toward brother, barely two; your hands paused
mid-clap.

Not much to say to each other. Disagreed
about almost everything, we did. Barely got through
a meal in peace. Barely got through.

When the cancer did its shimmy
up your bones, I used to feel so humble, so caved-
in by what I imagined to be
your unrelenting pain.

Even when you tried, Dad, words
were stiff in your mouth, crisp
as fresh bills. Silence was your speech.

When I think of you I want to crack
open the shuttered doors of lost
yet unforgettable language. My speech
is longing and I am longing for you, Dad,
to be held and hopeful again
in the tightly guarded
scrutiny of your love.

PAUL LE SAGE/POCATELLO

Hugh's Cafe (Cedar City, Utah)

Moccasins slide softly across
cafe floors as the lights dim in
the summer storm. The fans click on
waiting for a long drink, then off
unsatisfied. Outside, the daily news
from Salt Lake is carried over buildings,
and doorways are cleared of local gossip.
Shopkeepers begin to close and make their

way toward Hugh's where the ice crackles in
the glasses and ranchers sip the last hot
cups of coffee. It is early August when
the hot wind curls up and down the canyons
and cafe waitresses in crisp uniforms move
lightly like animals in the desert.

R. J. PETRILLO/POCATELLO

Weatherwise

Dried grasses bend to winter winds
that sweep in from all sides.
It couldn't be any other way;
grasses reckon weight of wind,
                 stem brushing stem.

My people rode shaggy dark horses
into the wind under weather skies,
eying the edge of prairie rise,
skirting wide coulees blown
stirrup deep with crusty snow.

They held no word for cold,
no curse for a cutbank camp
when light wearied of afternoon.
Wind moaning over grasslands
became the oath my people owned.

           * * * * *

When I was young, the people told
interwoven stories . . . tales
of prairie winters seeking patience,
of wind erasing final traces,
hinting at lessons yet to learn.

Don't take these words for gospel;
others who heard the stories spoken
still cling to wind as to some
tightly fashioned outer skin
of their own shrewd devising.

Weatherwise is bred-in-the-bone:
legacy where sure winds lean

and tracks commit to drifting snows
among red willows, dead grasses waving,
                    stem touching stem.

CHARLES POTTS/IDAHO FALLS

Alpiner

White Knob
and the trail leads
up Cliff Crik

to what was once
many peoples home

the mine here
silver and copper
cover the grave
of an infant uncle

what life must have been for
Charlie Rob
local gadabout
headbuster for
the IWW
a grandfather pulling
from the earth
a precious stench

but now there's only
part of an amethyst
bottle

Independence Missouri
stamped rite on the glass

2
the cabin of
Tommy Ding
one of Mackay's
mountain madmen

deer antlers
litter the yard
a catalog and
calendar
on the inside walls

skull of a hare
nailed on the door

3
we refold road maps
joked a friend
not far from where
the willows bend

at the Conoco station
on Custer Street
to the music of
his dancing feet

DIANE RAPTOSH/NAMPA

Just West of Now

My dad and all who've chopped the stalks
of corn to mix with hay remain
among those having still a higher
calling in this world; they've vowed
to stay out west for good. They view
this urge as one of sustenance
and livelihood—they'd sooner die

than think to leave. What *if* they live
with a firm resolve I'll always lack
about the place? I live convinced,
instead, that memory's the thing to keep
a place intact as is, *as was*,
or to arrange it as it never was
and never could be, which is what

I'd much prefer. In point of fact
my father has been gone for years
and never touched a scythe. He moved

west from Detroit and took
up golf. My uncle was the one
who bought up plots of land in Idaho,
bailed Dad out, then stayed.

What's more, I've heard these days
of pestilential hoppers eating livestock
feed and shrubs. When all is said
and done about the place even the Rockies
sometimes fall short, as they did
the time before the last time
I went home. The night before
I left again, the moon swayed

in a hammock and I lolled, thinking "What if
they *do* live for some higher kind
of good here? Next time, for sure,
I'll stay and let the real thing take
the place of reminiscence." And the baling
machine rose and fell, settling all
the fresh-cut into familial rows.

Idaho

In fields hay rigs
aim like telescopes
condensing mountain

ranges. Irrigation
pipes meander, casual
about distance. Carp

swim open-mouthed
in roadside canals,
following hunches

toward uncharted
waterways. In car
seats people scoot ahead

far as they can, as here
and there a finger
taps the highest peak.

VERN RUTSALA/MCCALL

Gravel, Roads, Fathers, Idaho, Hobos, Memory

We move slowly now over gravel,
the last hint we've had of roads
in this long search for our fathers.
We hope this place is Idaho
as we were told by hobos
so far back in memory

it's nearly lost. Or is this memory
we touch and only think it's gravel,
our path more lost than any hobo's?
Perhaps we've followed too many roads
as imaginary as the place called Idaho
where they said we would discover fathers.

But still we are without fathers
except those fading images in memory
who invented this wilderness of Idaho.
Soon enough we'll eat the gravel,
soon enough we'll abandon roads
and jungle-up forever with the hobos.

Or do we dream the hobos
as we dream our lost fathers,
night after night, along these roads?
There is something in our blood, a memory
grinding like gears to produce this gravel
we scatter like seeds all over Idaho.

Give us a break, we're lost, Idaho!
We can't even find those old hobos,
and quarry as we will there's too little gravel
for the single file we need to reach our fathers!
We're drunk, confused, our memory
bulldozed and gouged by new roads.

We travel circles, not roads
and have never admitted Idaho
to the union, much less our memory.
And we carry within us strange hobos

who all insist they are our fathers
in voices harsh as gravel.

So we give up roads and gravel
and every memory of dim hobos
who lied of Idaho and our fathers.

The Coast of Idaho

Late at night we heard waves
suffering their slow
way from Oregon,

crawling the dust like snails,
scaling mountains, scuffling
through gulches

until we felt them in the lake
where our monster drowsed
waiting for the perfect weekend

when he would make us famous
in a Sunday supplement.
He knew the sea

and in him we knew it too.
He was an exile
from that green regime

and now he farmed our lake
masquerading as a deadhead
winking those old knotholes

in the moon-inspired waves.
Winters he spooned the arctic in—
our dogs turned white,

our dark bears
erased themselves with snow—
but the sea was always there

lapping in that inch of air,
urged across all those miles
from Coos Bay,

moving like an oyster
then surfacing again with spring,
our scoop of sea

our pool of sky
containing all the images—
the green deep,

the giant bear-trap clams
of South Sea movies,
U-boat sharks

patrolling each dream,
water tigers, sea elephants
and the caped ray

cloud shadow, devil fish—
all piped into our lives
underground, by radio

and double features twice a week.
Our water glass vision
of the sea came in, a log

wearing a halloween mask,
calling our names in sleep,
pumping our blood all night.

Words

We had more than
we could use.
They embarrassed us,
our talk fuller than our
rooms. They named
nothing we could see—
dining room, study,
mantel piece, lobster

thermidor. They named
things you only
saw in movies—
the thin flicker Friday
nights that made us
feel empty in the cold
as we walked home
through our only great
abundance, snow.
This is why we said 'ain't'
and 'he don't.'
We wanted words to fit
our cold linoleum,
our oil lamps, our
outhouse. We knew
better but it was wrong
to use a language
that named ghosts,
nothing you could touch.

RICHARD SHELTON/BOISE

On Lake Pend Oreille

All day the wind has made love
to the lake and tonight the water
takes up its bruises and moves
away to a safer distance.

I am listening for the small
sounds of another departure.

Summer is leaving
as if she could afford the trip.
She stands by the road
in her ragged coat and fumbles
for her keys in the darkness.

At her pathetic signal
the aristocracy of leaves
will begin to let go.

Harry Orchard

You lived out of town where the land
sloped up to Table Rock. The prison
looked exactly as a prison should,
except for the roses in front: walls
of granite blocks held together
by their own weight and our fear.
We didn't know what went on in there;
we didn't want to know. The river
kept running. Summer brought heat,
winter brought snow. The grounds
outside the prison were always neat
and the roses were magnificent.

Because of you I grew up thinking prisons
were places outside town where men
who had the knack for it retired
to tend their roses. I was a child
when I first heard your name, and I
thought you had always been an old man
with a cane who came out and knelt down
stiffly, like in church, among the flowers.
And I thought, because you were so good
at growing things, they named an avenue
in our town, *Orchard*, after you.

When you and the state were young
you were convicted of placing a bomb
on the Governor's gate. He came home
and opened it; it was the last gate
he ever opened. There had been a fight
between miners and the owners of the mines.
You were labor. The Governor was on the side
of management. It's strange how times
and governors don't seem to change.

I don't know whether or not you did it;
but I can imagine you hiding among the vines
which covered the wall outside his mansion,
young and terrified, with sticks of dynamite
like a bouquet in your hands. That was
the picture the state's lawyers painted,

but there were questions about who hired you,
questions about two union bosses and a lawyer.
Somebody paid to shut those questions up.

And what did you do? Oh, Harry! Harry!
You know what you did. You got religion
in the county jail, and when they brought
you to the trial, forgave them all: forgave
the union bosses and the owners of the mines,
forgave the State Militia for their guns,
forgave the men who built the bullpen
at Coeur d'Alene, forgave the striking miners
who starved in it, forgave the Governor,
forgave the crooked lawyers, forgave everyone.
You took it on yourself and praised the Lord,
and even Clarence Darrow couldn't help you then.

Harry Orchard, you lived in prison so long
that when they offered you a pardon in old age,
you refused it. By then you couldn't give
the garden up. And I believe that rumor
later said about the prisoners whose bodies
disappeared after they were beat to death
or died from lack of care, how they were buried
by guards after dark in a place no one would
suspect or dare desecrate. How many
left their cells to feed the flowers?

And I see you still. It is late afternoon.
You are kneeling in a flower bed, a trowel
in your hand, while all your roses flame.

We always build our prisons out of town
so we don't have to look at them. But we
saw yours. Whole families of us drove
out there to see your roses bloom. We also
saw the statue of the Governor, downtown
in front of the State Capitol, its head
and shoulders white with pigeon drippings.
It's still there, on a traffic island.
Only tourists look at it, and never more
than once. At its base some scraggly roses
grow with yellow leaves and hardly any bloom.
Some things even the state can't do.

Harry Orchard, there stands the Governor
with an iron jaw, squat, menacing,
the ugliest thing a schoolboy ever saw.
Somebody blew him up and he went
into the history book we had to read,
but we could never remember his name.
Harry Orchard, we remember yours
because for over fifty years
outside the gates of Hell you grew
the most beautiful roses in all Idaho.
When you died, you went straight into fame.

ONA SIPORIN/BOISE

Boise: The Woman Who Loved Birds

Had a passion for flight.
Had only to step outside into the evening
air to know this
exaltation, to let go.

In her children's cries
she heard the gulls',
certain every moment
held a transformation.

Walking the ridge at Camel's Back Park
the call of canada geese pierced the fog.
Hearing this her heart would lift
heavy, awkward at first as a pelican,
then, reaching its element, turn
graceful, circling the small spot
of earth where she walked.

The woman who loved birds could laugh
away the fool of her human self
simply by walking toward the waning West,
simply looking up she was magic:

a swallow, gliding;
a hawk, live arrow on its way to some blood red heart.
Witch, angel or simply woman?

She could not know.
Only this—these were the moments when
both she and the earth let go.

After the Death of the Magician

The labor of night was to separate herself
from the vision of day, and the day to come,
was to walk in darkness to the center
of the harvested field,
and there, without song, or sight, or touch,
to wrap the length and width of the night around her
and sleep and rise again.
He, who in death had become
the idea of love,
was to be stilled, at peace.

She was to learn this,
the magician's final trick:
to erase the flesh, to disappear
into the darkness
and then, by day, become again a whole woman.

BILL SIVERLY/LEWISTON

Lewiston

His first real town was nothing much
A small river city just big enough
To house a smug bourgeois. Kulaks mostly
Loggers and cowboys. Named after Meriwether Lewis
Who offered his life to serve mankind
Then shot himself at 35 on the Natchez Trace.
Meanwhile the Kid
Found Lewiston about what he expected
Dozing through the oppressive summer of 1950
Flags limp on the Fourth of July.
Before the pulp and paper mill
Polluted the town with management and labor.
Before the Army Corps of Engineers refashioned the river
by means of a dam as big as the hand of God.

By 1964 the Kid was desperate
Afraid he was stuck forever with nothing
But the image of the grail. Forever
Staring out a window like the dead
At those implacable bronze hills.

GINO SKY/BOISE

Gospel Hump

I rose out the cab like a velvet
pickup of american baby blues
with my chromed rig buffalo beer
and high school steady indian girl
driving me hot out at nineteen cents
a gallon from Pocatello through
every western novel of shotgun
marriages and backseat divorces
and I didn't know what it was that
ghosted the road except that
there was a thousand miles of indian
towns and cowboy bars where I winged
the sweep along those hunkered
streams and everything was gospel
so long as gasoline and dreams
were as easy as carnival girls.

JOHN F. SOLLERS/BOISE

An Eye to the Cold

The constant rage of wind made it so cold
that fence-hung icicles slanted south
almost horizontal. Snow smoke whipped
in banners across fields
and built drifts so deep in spots
that school buses couldn't buck them.

At seventeen, I looked through bouquets
of blue-grey frost flowers in opaque windows
wishing that Sheila Redding had hypothermia

and I was there with a fox fur blanket
and my skin to warm the goose flesh
up her thighs.

Perpetua

Hands flat against the epidermis
of still water feel tension of fish fins
rise from sifting sand, rise from pebbles
rolling through sand, against boulders, rise
a thin film over water, rise and seep, left
hand, right hand, rise and hang, Pacific
mist, rise and pull sky from water, rise
and push car claw, dog fang, rise and clash
a charivari of broken glass, rise and fall
heron plucks the eye from frog, rise
and settle, a thin layer of salt in pores
of bleached bone.

Rosie's Ghost

When he was ten, the goats
tripped by, bleating into their places.
He collar-chained each in her turn
on a high hoof-worn platform.
Two leathery teats spat milk,
sweet warm, sweet warm,
tingling on stainless steel.
Then he let them out.

One morning, wrapped in a dream
of spearing carp in river shallows,
yellow fins thrashing,
he forgot to set them free.

Closed in and panicked, Rosie leaped
from the platform and died
in the collar-chain noose.

On river rock, spear high,
he remembered too late. He ran

back to lift her bulk
and make things right
like it was only a bad dream.
But her eyes never blinked.

He and his father bore her,
pulleyed her hind feet first
up a Russian olive,
butchered her out.

The boy nailed the hide on the barn wall,
carted guts, hooves amd head to a hole.
A kerplop of dirt covered the eyes.

In gray dawns and evenings
when he opened the gate,
rattling pails at milking time,
her white head, chin whiskers and brown eyes
hovered over sage and lichened lava.

After thirty years, in alley shadows
by garbage cans near lilacs
she resurrects and
catches in his throat.

KIM STAFFORD/POCATELLO

Pocatello Town

Late one night in Walltown the boys were playing cards,
Sipping at their whiskey, smoking their cigars.
Says a cowboy, "Boys, I'm out of chuck. I'd best throw in
    my hand.
I've lost my horse, lost my hat. I've lost the means to
    stand
    in Pocatello, Pocatello town."

The Doctor says, "Now Sammy, you need not leave the
    game.
You need not quit the table and walk our streets in shame.
For I have a wager that I will offer you:

Ten dollars against your body, when your long life is
    through
        in Pocatello, Pocatello town."

Says Sammy, "That's a wager that I will not refuse,
But I'll surely quit this country if I should chance to lose.
You'll never get my body, when my long life is through!"
The Doctor said, "Upon your foot I'd put a small tattoo:
    Pocatello, Pocatello Town".

Well, the cowboy took the wager—his hands and face
    were pale.
The room was thick and blue with smoke, the whiskey
    tasted stale.
When the cowboy drew a set of queens, their faces looked
    so kind
Till the Doctor showed his aces and all the room went
    blind
        in Pocatello, Pocatello town.

The Doctor hired the barber next morning all so soon
To grind him up some coaldust at the back of the saloon;
To take a red-hot needle and dip it in the grounds,
To prick two names on Sam's left foot—the Doctor's and
    the town's:
        Pocatello, Pocatello town.

The cowboy left that morning, nobody saw him go.
He must have hopped a boxcar where his tracks stopped
    in the snow.
"He's got away," the boys all said. The Doctor said, "I'll
    wait.
He may have left by boxcar; he'll come back home by
    freight
        to Pocatello, Pocatello town."

The section-hands saw Sammy as he rolled out through
    Shoshone.
They glimpsed him last in Boise when he rolled on west
    alone.

The sun goes up, the sun goes down. The trains, they
    come and go.
The Doctor's waiting for a call from the OSL Depot
    in Pocatello, Pocatello town.

It's thirteen years in April when the buds break in the
    trees.
The freightman calls the Doctor about a coffin C.O.D.
But the Doctor'd died the night before. Since neither had
    much kin
They laid them two men side by side as they threw them
    cold clods in,
    in Pocatello, Pocatello town.

Now Walltown's gone in Poky, where the cowboy lost his
    bet.
They've built the courthouse on that spot, right where that
    cathouse set.
Instead of cards and whiskey now, they talk about the law,
And how to steal with statutes instead of five-card draw,
    in Pocatello, Pocatello town.

Juliaetta Coffee Blues

My old truck broke down at the edge of town—
I turn the key, she don't make a sound.
I'll be walking along the highway late tonight.
I step into a cafe to pass the time:
Grade B, that's friendly, coffee's a dime,
A cup of sweet coffee stirred with a silver spoon.

Now there's a warmth that's left in a coffee cup
When the coffee's been all drunk up,
So my heart still holds a memory of you.
That sweet black coffee is all drunk dry,
Just the grounds I'm chewing is left behind
And I'm hunched here holding the cold cup
                of my heart.

I put a pack of sugar in my pocket for the road,
Better take two—if only I'd knowed
What a woman can do to a man when he's all alone.

I tried you with sugar, tried you with cream,
Baby, I could use a warm-up, if you know what I mean
Because I'm hunched here holding the cold cup
                     of my heart.

That cafe counter is all scrubbed down.
I got to hold a cup now that you left town
And your hand won't reach my way, no more now.
The waitress says, "Honey, it's time to close,"
I start walking like the wind that blows
Down a street that's dark and lonely as a man can be.

I put a pack of sugar in my pocket for tonight,
Out on the highway when the stars are bright
And that cold wind starts whistling through my bones.
I thought I saw some headlights' far-off glow,
But it's only the moon shining through the snow
Where I'm standing in the gravel trying to hitchhike
                     on the wind.

But there's a warmth in a coffee cup
When the coffee's been all drunk up,
So my heart still holds a memory of you.
That sweet black coffee is all drunk dry,
Just the grounds I'm chewing is left behind
And I'm hunched here holding the cold—
      but that's an old story by now,
      so old it's just about worn away.

Villanelle for the Spiders

The smallest weavers work at night
To link together all they know
And build their web that holds our light.

It's drops of dew that catch my sight
And tell me, when through dawn I go,
That smallest weavers work at night.

I find the spiral fabric slight
And wonder how they spin so slow
Yet build their web that holds our light.

A touch could tear, my deep breath might
Destroy the net their trust put low,
For smallest weavers work at night.

Patience is life and their delight,
Ready again if wind should blow
To build their web that holds our light.

Our feeble threads are strung so tight
Across the darkness deep below.
The smallest weavers work at night
To build their web that holds our light.

PAUL E. TRACY/CALDWELL

Existentialist

On Malheur's searing lots
The horned toad squats.

He gets along
Without iced drinks, or song.

To anneal his hands and feet in this heat
He stops beneath a sage and blinks
The same as anyone who thinks.

He, too,
Has toyed with Philosophy. "Out of the Void
I came. Into the Void I go. Reluctantly.
I do not understand this silent land.
Nor does this land know me.
Why am I Here?
Why am I not out There?"

So, throughout Time
He continues to stare . . . to rest
On his tiny fists, and his sunburned
Wrists.
e.g., he exists.

GEORGE VENN/SPIRIT LAKE

How to Live Two Days in Osburn, Idaho

Dredge, the Welshman, drunk again
wants to hear a steel-driving song,
says get down to yourself and sing.
"Don't stop now—both feet in the air."
You have to play for him.

The seedling in the yard grows in
a cage. Protection is the school.
By the greenhouse, girls dance on a fence,
laughing at the mudchuckholed street.
You have to play for them.

At the Emerald Empire Motel, a woman sweeps.
She knows the room's not much,
but the sheets are clean. You can use her
phone for local calls, that's all.
You play up to her.

The miner watches his son pick grounders
on the dirt diamond. He talks big fights,
smokes his pipe inside his pickup cab.
They're all hard-hit liners here. To know,
just play third a while.

The Lions at the Lion's Club don't roar
without another drink bought loudly by
the local editor, named Penny, who's
got a copper head that's a company ante.
You play hob with them, not poker.

The girls in Wallace at the Lux will
ask you to their rooms. They thought you'd
left their Coeur d'Alene the day those
kids ran Ballet Folk out of town.
You play fast and loose with them.

The woman from Burke who's eighty-two
says she's the only one left alive
in her family. She brings down a diary,
wants to salvage her own brief history.
Play straight with her.

Your teeth ache, remember the mines
a mile deep. Sunshine's not a friend here,
and Bunker Hill's a war. These men dig all
the silver, and they are always poor.
At work, you ply these words for them,

for anyone patching scraps and fog together
between a year of strikes and bad weather,
for anyone planting tomatoes by the slag heap
by the river running clean again this year.
Just make this play for them all.

Be the two-day singer in this town.
Wait for them to come for coffee in this cafe;
listen carefully and stare up the canyon.
When they go, write this in the streets
and play fair, by god, with every voice you hear.

LYNN WIKLE/BOISE

A Handmaiden Speaks

A Serb or Bulgarian woman, looking for variety in love,
will wash in wine or water the copper coins from a dead
man's eyes and give her husband the solution to drink that
he may be rendered blind to her adventures.
        —Funk & Wagnall

Now that she is blond and pleased
with her own breasts, our lady carries

a satchel of red flowers, not the wine
in which she has steeped two corpse coins

for her husband. He sits in a white room
blind as the dead. Bits of fire clink

within the silver flask she wraps
in a deer's dampened skin. Her nipples

are vivid as gold. Even the hibiscus
isn't her equal. Under her, the bed skitters,

grows crumpled horns, scatters itself
across three breakers. She smooths

her sleeves and speaks, indirectly,
as women do, praising the fullness

of a certain word, another's bite.
We listen to what she does not say

most carefully, search the shadows
under leaves for food fine enough to serve.

The Changeling's Mother

I am your new mother
but I'm not ugly.
Upstairs, in the rooms
where you are not allowed
where the closets are filled
with shimmering things
I scent my skin
to make your father crazy
and paint my eyes the old way
to drive him blind.

I have secret names.
One of them sounds like rocks
tumbling down cliffs at night—
one of them like the tide, leaving.
Even when you know their sounds
you can't stop them.
You will sleep
in the cold room downstairs.
You will go to bed before dark.

I'll prepare you odd dishes
with saffrons and curries
and you will eat
what is set before you.
You will be courteous
at this table, mindful
of your father's sacrifice

or you will be sent away
to eat with the dogs.

This will help you
to remember your manners.
You will use your napkin
and keep your elbows to yourself.
You will not dawdle over your plate.
In this house
we do not play with what we eat.
We hold our forks thusly.
With our other hand, just so,
we hold our knives.

CHARLES DAVID WRIGHT/BOISE

The Foolhen
(or Spruce Grouse)

If not cutthroat but grouse were my game,
I could take you just where you are
here in Murdoch Creek on the path
between me and the next chancy pool.
You are the most unlikely thing alive
the way you squat blankly and neither hide nor run
unless you're pushed, as I might now with the tip
of my rod. Most of us half expect
some heavy hand from behind, and learn to be
fierce or devious or fast, tasteless or tactless.
I have been all of them, whatever works
against whatever's coming. What do you think,
are you too insignificant for tragedy?
Do deskclerks never get leukemia
or plain widows take a wrong turn
or seed dealers get a collect call in the night?
Or are all dodges useless, since we never know
where it's coming from?
                              You are a dumb bird
I hope, and I'd like you to know
from where we stand how easily
I could wring your neck.

Shaving

When his match, when his match kept missing
his pipe, I knew from my father's face,
sharp grey stobs in a cornfield reaped and dry,
he hadn't begun a beard out of an old man's right
or November whimsy, but that his hands were going.
Watching him there fumbling the light again,
I went back to another Sunday with him
when on small boy's legs I fell behind him
in the snow going to church. He came back for me
laughing, and boosted me to his chest. My cheeks
touched then two smoothnesses at once,
the velvet collar of his Lord Chesterfield
and the warm plains of his best Sunday face.
I lit his pipe and said, "Smoke that while I shave you
for Sunday." He sat on the toilet seat like
a good boy taking medicine. My fingers
touched through the lather the cleft of his chin
and the blade made pink and blue swaths
in the snowy foam, and we were done.
Pretending to test, I bent down my cheek to his
a moment, and then we went to church.

There Comes a Wind

There comes a wind
just when you begin to think winter
might allow a slow melon or some lingering plums
like the late years of wise, splendid women.
You woke to half the leaves laid down
like cherished postcards on the album street.
Did you think that was the wind?
That was not the wind. There comes
a wind that harps on the chickenwire,
that strews the roosters, blows out every light
of recollection, that makes leaning
the only way to go, that sloughs tumbleweed
against the door, dry derelicts.
It takes the field and makes the cows face it
and you face it. Fall left something.
That blows away. That was the wind.

⚘ The Contemporaries

Introduction

THE MOST DIFFICULT SECTION OF THIS ANTHOLOGY, FROM AN EDI-
torial standpoint, has been this one, which comprises the work of
some sixty poets currently living and writing in the state. We believe
the following work exemplifies the best poetry being written in Idaho
today, but of course we recognize that no collection of this sort can
claim to be complete or definitive. Despite our awareness of the
many and varied literary activities in the state, we have probably
overlooked some of Idaho's poets, but if so, it has not been from lack
of effort. We are well aware, for example, of such organizations as the
Gem State Writers Guild and the Idaho Writers League, and we
know of many active local writing groups throughout the state.

Our anthology scarcely scratches the surface of the fine poems
which have appeared in various literary or "little" magazines throughout the state, from the independent *Red Neck Review of Literature*,
edited by Penelope Reedy in Fairfield, to the recently started *Para-
dise Creek Journal*, a campus literary magazine at the University of
Idaho. *Rendezvous*, a journal of arts and letters, has been published
at Idaho State University for more than twenty years now, and Boise
State University's *Cold-Drill* has won prizes several times as an un-
dergraduate literary magazine. William Studebaker edited a literary
magazine called *Sawtooth* out of the College of Southern Idaho for
several years, Ron McFarland's *Snapdragon* ran for ten years (1977–
1987) out of the University of Idaho, and M. K. Browning published
Slackwater Review for nearly ten years out of Lewis-Clark State College. Fay Wright and Chad Klinger have developed an increasingly
impressive magazine at North Idaho College with the *Trestle Creek
Review*. Poems by Idaho writers also appear in such diverse publications as the *Idaho Arts Journal*, *Idaho English Journal*, *Idaho Li-
brarian*, and *Boise Magazine*. In the fall of 1988 the University of
Idaho embarked upon a new literary magazine entitled *The Idaho*.

The above listing still accounts for only a part of what has trans-
pired and what is underway with respect to poetry in Idaho. Ahsahta
Press at Boise State University and Confluence Press at Lewis-Clark
State College have published distinguished series of poetry collections. Independent editors, including Richard Ardinger of Limber-

lost Press (Boise), Harald Wyndham of Blue Scarab Press (Pocatello), Bill Roth and Carolyn Gravelle of Two Magpie Press in Kendrick, and Donnell Hunter of Honeybrook Press in Rexburg, have also published individual collections of poems, as well as broadsides, often with genuine love and understanding of the printer's art.

Creative writing programs at the state's junior colleges, colleges, and universities have brought in renowned visiting poets for workshops and readings in addition to supporting the work of young writers. The Whittenberger Foundation in Caldwell has helped support poetry writing in the public schools, and a major boost to creative writing was provided with the creation of the State Writer-in-Residence program in 1984, funded by the Idaho Commission on the Arts. Three poets in this section have occupied or are occupying the latter position: Ron McFarland (1984–85), Robert Wrigley (1986–87), and Eberle Umbach (1988–89).

It is probably inevitable that the largest cities in the state and those which are college or university centers would account for more poems in this anthology than the smaller towns, but we were pleased to find that this section lists poets from more than two dozen cities and towns throughout Idaho. The poems are printed as in the previous section, alphabetically by the poet's name. Some of the poems in this section have appeared previously in refereed literary magazines as diverse as *Kayak* and the *Christian Science Monitor*, in anthologies, or in individual collections, but most are published here for the first time.

The Contemporaries

MARGARET AHO/POCATELLO

Carpal Bones

What is unspoken,
wordless,
lives between the fingers
and the forearm,
in the pale throats of the wrists
which swallow so much
and are wise. Here
eight small bones
absorb, radiate what
can't be said.
In the dark, where I
extend my hands,
they give off a clustered light
like a second brain, like
an ovum
already fertile and
eight-celled.
In a fairy tale
a maiden's hands are sometimes severed
and this clump of bones
is snatched,
separated like dwarf-iris
bulbs, shaken, thrown,
consulted.

Pause at Forty

November is not deaf
despite its losses,
despite swallows
threaded on phone wires
like black counters,
like an abacus whose beads
bunch wing to wing
with here and there a space

between fragilities, a pause
revealing not
a sum
or difference,
but the presence of a live
wire, the prolongation of a certain
sound,
heard
and held firm.

DOUGLAS AIRMET/BLACKFOOT

Presence

over my face
your fingers
trace quietly

the southern cross
sailors have seen
my eyes wide open

at the tale
your two hands
tell on me

startled
from my hemisphere
I turn

like a deer
lifting its head
to look

at a rustle
how still
it looks

it remains
after the noise
of arrival departs

it turns
to the grass
again

and feeds
in the presence
of danger

quietly
you take me
out of myself

RICHARD ARDINGER/BOISE

One Place for Another

memory trickles
like a map, red and blue,
toward the lull
of a familiar face,
a youthful mouth
you knew, the scent
of a woman no longer
around, though the road
to her home still
curves and turns
through the naked
eyes of a photograph,
or perhaps the sound
of rain, a downpour
flattening forest
leaves, or the way
the moon rose once
and never again
through the webbed
reach of trees,
red-blooded and full,
over the bed of a lover,
rivers that run through
your blood like lust,
mountains that crawl

into memory, maps
that chart brittle
assurances of hope
and call the roads
that limp off into distances
home.

Planting Day
—for rosemary

she walks barefoot,
bent in the garden, poking
seeds and molding mounds
of soft wet earth
for cucumbers. snow
still caps the mountains
as she stakes tomatoes
and peppers perfect
with yellow ribbon,
ties sticks in a makeshift
fence against dogs
and rabbits and to make
it pretty, marks rows
with seed packets,
measures time in inches.
she knows how soon
weeds thicken, rounded
mounds erode, vines
strangle crooked fences,
and ball jars boil
september in the kitchen.
she'd like to pickle
the moon in its own
rhythms, shelve the sun
like honey, or just
hold planting day
inside a locket's memory
raging forever
with crickets.

Report from More's Creek

You should be here.
We sit up late on the porch
each night to gawk at stars
and eye Mars even closer,
checking headlines every morning
to see if anyone knows.
The weather obliges. Broke,
we read books, Bate's biography
of Keats, Stegner's *Angle of Repose*,
Harrison's *Farmer*,
all the poets, even Weldon Kees.
Grasshoppers climb the kitchen window
like magnified microbes on a slide.
The barn's gone giddy with swallows.
The dog sleeps through
the errant rooster's croon at noon,
and the long grass rages for rain.
Each day we chisel mountains
with our eyes, keep a clean edge
on the sky.

In Another Country
—for Nancy Stringfellow

We draw out palpable words
and set them free, birds
igniting on the tongue.
We loll in language we acquire
along the way and pass along,
learn by saying
what we have to say, hands
aflutter in the room.

The meadowlarks, the skittery
finches, the frogs are up
from the mud. The long grass
loves the wind again, and
begging buds are open
mouths to sun.

The earth's all roots and seeds
we want to plant our feet
among, let our eyes grow green
with envy at what our words
are blinded by when we lift
our faces to the spattering rain
and clouds boil blue what we know.

DIANA ARMSTRONG/MOSCOW

Spring Spell

My marish spring blood
aching with barns is racing.
By my pulse you can tell April.
Unlike the moon I am wanton
in the narrow pen of my arc.

I take heart from crocus
who take the risk of bloom.
No choice but to throw
their spears upward, unfurl.

Cousin to hot-blooded bulbs
and horses I say You,
come to my room, my heat
my houseful of rooms to fill.

KATHLEEN ARMSTRONG/WENDELL

False Dusk

You call me to summer and the liar sky
where birds, a kind of hawk, you think,
are angling through the trees.

We watch.
They glide and stammer
in the storm's false dark,
struggling up

as though the evening held them down,
then swoop to snatch
at something we can't see.

You draw me close.
We stand as one, and, suddenly,
I want to tell you—
the heights are a delusion after all.
Those men, the ones in other towns,
the loving nights that started with good-bye—
they were you. They all were you.

This is the poem I said I'd never write.
But standing here in the fading light,
bound by your arms
and the wisdom of the ground,
I must look up
and, looking up, recall
the tilt and tremble
of the flight that brought me here,
deceived and frightened
by the narrowing sky.

The Hunter

Something in the blood, this dark urgency
that drives him shivering from his sleep

who stumbles fiercely into morning
whose wife stirs now toward the warm hollow

of his absence, sleep grumbling from her mouth
a sweeter kind of death between her legs.

He settles in his skin and he begins
alone in darkness, first through rain, then snow

past the lake, past the orchard where summer
hangs rotting on the branch, to the mountains

into first light, out of his life, his meaning
face to the wind. He tries for musk, for tracks

for the sound of game breaking through the brush.
It's his own scent he's after, and the tracks

he follows are his own. For his hunger
is older than his reasons; his reasons

older than these mountains which hide him now
from the hunter who stalks him, who has him

in his sights, who is ready for the kill
who is himself, the hunter in his blood.

LEA BAECHLER/MOSCOW

Chase Lake

In the morning we push off
from beneath the low branches of bent pines
and paddle slowly into shadows where the sun
has not yet come, staying close

to shore, within reach of the dark, shallow water.
And so we begin the swift dip
of our paddles deep and sure and their lift
clean out of the lake, the invisible sound

of our muscles stretching as the left hand takes
the paddle from the right in a silent arc
of sunlight. We breathe deeply, try to find,
before I tire first, the rhythm of our separate

strength. The small tests of quiet:
to hook the paddle's blade at my feet
into the curve of the canoe, the handle resting
at my right side lightly on the seat, and lift

the rod back, casting out until the purple
water dog hits with a quick hiss at the edge
of a lily pad, your paddle trailing noiselessly
just beneath the surface through the red-stemmed weeds.

All morning we keep that quiet, speak only
with glance and nod, a slight shift, the paddles
feathering the water, the canoe drifting. Even afterwards
the stories fishermen tell at night in camp or later

back at the bar with others are serious stuff
about right spots and good holes, times of day,
bait, lures, the incredible catch and
the almost incredible catch, the varieties

of elemental suffering that go with weather
and bad luck. There's a cult of silence about
fishing time: what happens when light reflects
from the wet paddles above us or what we see

in the hours of lily pads, the swamp grass
at their edge, the beaver dam on the south shore,
the jagged shadow of pine mountains
still before the mid-morning wind rises.

Taking a Life

I am teaching my niece to jump waves and tumble
in the ocean. She is five and when she goes home
at night she wants to lie in my arms and sing
all the songs she knows. All summer into fall
I write every day, 117 unmailed letters
beneath the same sky that itself does not know
the distance of one shoreline to another.
A thin wire hums behind my eyes, each word,
each letter like Chinese water torture:
a willing submission. I want to believe

that words somehow have a life of their own,
can sing inviolate and reach beyond the grave
consequence of one stroke, the black elongated
"l" of love, the cursive letter looping back
on itself. In our language it's no accident
that love begins with a self-reflective gesture.
It is said that wisdom comes with suffering.
I can't see it. If I take my life back now

it's not because I am healed or because
I understand something. The sky is there
through the window each morning, whether a blue
thinned by cold light or the grey that comes
with a sleet my bones are made of.
My friend writes *my twelve-year-old daughter
has given up on living* and I lie awake nights
for my friend and for Liza. There are planes
I fly on from time to time, as usual; the moon
hangs in the backyards of our mothers.

My three-year-old nephew makes up a poem
and with a bright wet face he tells me *Someone
has trees in their garden and someone has bees
in their garden; someone has plants in their garden
and someone has ants in their garden; someone has
little boys and toys and noise in their garden*
and he has more. It's a small thing,
and merciful, how we retract and curve back out
again, and it has nothing to do with any one thing
we understand or could ever explain.

KIM BARNES/LEWISTON

Women at the Wash Stand

The women laundered
great loads of gray
cotton, red flannel, heavy
black pants cut short, clear
of snags and saws. Pockets
turned out pine needles, tamarack
bark gold as medallions.
Above the bleach-eaten boards
the wringer-washer sat
like a white toad, all belly
and noise. I stood eye-level
with the twin rollers, watched
thin wafers of cloth
drop to the basket below. Hands
worked close, inches

from the grinding. The veins
of wrists hung above
the wet material, blue
streamers against white
sky, thin and delicate,
or chickens' feet, talons
of blood working a spell
through the tight cotton weave,
worked to the washer's rough
chanting, a witch's trick,
enchantment, iron legs, steel arms, neck
and chest of granite, delicate dance
of falling trees, saws frozen cold
as winter fog: *Let them come back*
in soft dust of pine, red fir splinters
stuck in amber, fronds
of forest fern dropping to the floor,
tea leaves of good omen.

Infestation

Behind Jensen's house
we found the den in the heart
of rock, each neat knot
a sheen of eyes,
a ticker-tape gone wild
in a pile of bad news.
We didn't know what to do
then, the slow rasp
of rattle growing beneath
our feet, spreading through
loose rock, ribbons
of sound that wove
around us, crawled the spine
of our fear until we bowed,
taken by the voice
we always knew would come:
soft chant of hornets, nests
and webs that hold
even after the bones
run dry with dust.

It's the fine silk
of lives, the infestation
spreading away from us
like honey, blood, love
from the den of the heart.

RUTH BULL/MOSCOW

Boom Town

Panting trucks nip at my bumper
all the way from Salt Lake to Vernal,
the highway a big city Front Street
dropped by mistake
in a hot strip through nowhere.

Last time I saw Vernal, it stretched out
asleep just east of the KOA.
Now it's a plastic
hamburger joint main street.
Four-wheel-drives with roll bars
paw at the tar like horny bulls,
gun down the double drag strip main street
Hellbent for the end of town before the shale oil
runs out,
the smell of tough money on their haunches.

Outside of town a slick of oil spawn
spatters across the sagebrush flats,
field welding, crane service, petrochemicals
a weed filled yard with a sign out front
Zoned Commercial.
Magpies sit on high tension wires,
wait for carrion.

Down a cracked sidewalk
a trail of oil
left by motorcycles
leads to a back street where pale children
play on the pavement to the sound of music
blaring through a slack screen door.

A pink woman
framed inside uncurtained windows
smiles on the video screen.
The people next door with their manicured yard
and flowers
sit inside and remember
how the town was
before.

The Red Dress

There is nothing decent about a leaving.
The decent thing, of course,
is not to go. I see the eagle soaring.
He comes off the hills in the first downdrafts of morning
his beak rapacious.
Will he lie down with the lion and the lamb
exchange his wings for the paws of a mouse?

The good wife
lays herself down on the pyre.
To extinguish herself is the mark of love
and twice the ash.

What do I bring you that I should stay?
The gift of my life for yours—this is my body
broken for you—something
to match your own brokenness.

By the roadside the grass is dried.
Its tassels brush yellow and bronze against the passing oak.
How beautiful its last days.
Grouse fly up from the elder, and the aspen leaves
rattle against the burning of chaff.

Your fingers reach now for my life.
I did not know how much of love
was fear or cold or faintness.

Along the road the sumac is red.
Does it know there will be another living?

I want to buy a red dress and wash my hair
to walk in the cool air
dressed in the softness of wool
to know the touch of apples and the smell of willow.
To wear a red dress the color of sumac
and my hair, shining.

KEVIN BUSHMAN/BURLEY

Good Morning

Fresh bacon crackles in an oval pan
That straddles the glowing burner
Like a rooster in an elm tree.
Smoky odors awaken and stretch their filmy arms,
Fly about the room like great grey bats
Until they tire and hang sleeping near the ceiling.
Coffee hiccups in a cow brown pot.

I lumber down the wooden stairs to the kitchen,
A pajama-clad black bear
Grit sticking to my slippered paws.
I'm dancing . . .
I'm Gene Kelly
Soft shoeing towards breakfast.

Idaho Christmas

> "Sometimes I think of home as
> storehouse, the more/ we leave
> behind, the less/ you say. The
> last time/ I couldn't take anything."
> Tess Gallagher

Behind an angry yellow cloud of smoke
I sit
On a taped-up red bar stool
Where Billy the Kid might have once outlined
His next chapter of Utah's sagebrush past.

This, the same tilted pole
Later occupied (I'm told)
By an underling of John Dillinger
Who laid his notched pistol
Upon this same broken pine bar
To satisfy the curiosity
Of some silage beet farmer
From Idaho Falls.

Red, yellow, green, blinking lights
Snake their way around the huge
Cracked oval mirror.
They remind me that it's Christmas.

Stool,
you remind me,
I am not home.

NADINE CHAPMAN/FERDINAND

On Solitude

Woman washing tiles,
each day you come
to the convent's walkway,
splash your holy water
upon a baked brick
landscape. Some laugh
at cracks that gleam
out penance in the face
of wise men's dirty feet,
or frown at wasted work.
Sisters even call you "fool"
—try to reason life
off reddened knees.
Your eyes rise up
from cushions of advanced age,
calling back accusers;
though you never speak,
many listen on the hidden
stairwells of your labor.

PETE CRUZ/KAMIAH

Indian Poker

Yes, she says, we're all sitting here
at three o'clock in the morning, each
holding one card to our forehead. Uncle Jaime
walks by quietly to get a drink and let us
know we are keeping him up
with our laughter. We see each
other's faces, but not our own,
and bet pennies on expressions,
bluffing sometimes.

I wake up often and don't look
at my face and on those mornings
I can still see Vicki's and hear her
saying, what do I know,
I'm just a blonde. Before she left
I bet she had time
to look in the rearview mirror
and check her face
or her hair.

But some mornings, no game
can hide my features. Each
gesture I saw in her face, that morning,
and behind her eyes as she looked down
in mock self-consciousness, was my own.
And even if I could see hers,
I wouldn't know which one of us was bluffing.

CHRISTINE OLSON DAVIS/NEW MEADOWS

The Little Mud

Green, the river feeds
the grass, slides under
willows, curls over rocks,
leans against a muddy
curve. October leaves
dapple the water's skin.

They waltz, circling in
and out of shadow, rest
against a dark soaked
branch, turn to glide
beneath the bridge.
Downstream, a Speckled Brown
waits below the surface
to surprise a stone-fly
nymph. It hangs, a blink
of silver in a black pocket.

ZEOMA DVORAK/MOSCOW

The Story Teller

we bury our dead; ribs to the sky
                a harp of the winds.
        the cries of the weeping
                hold up the clouds.

deep blue eyes cannot reflect high circling
        birds that knew him.

the young remember an old man sitting on
        aged haunches; a balancing
                of mind and body,
        long grey hair pulled tightly, folded
                back against itself
                wrapped with bright red cloth,
        like a crimson bird perched
                on his neck.
palms cupping sharp knees, fingers point
        downward; wait to express in the air:
                two sun-colored fish fight upstream,
                        he tells of their beginning, of
                                their dying.
                hands whirl as a dust spirit
                        sweeping the desert floor,
                touches a familiar face to trace a line
                a quick clap becomes the sound of a branch
                                snaps underfoot,
sparkling words: the veiling falls hide unknown caves.

places deer left bark curls off trees
    and tiny pools of water held in a footprint
    he knew of their passing; they watched his.

children left the circle with words still
    drawing pictures in their minds;
        small tribes pocketed in coves beyond
            their mountains,
    a weaving of colors they had never seen!
    dreams of creatures from deep dark
        waters, with fins like great blue
          wings, breaking the surface.

the old remember him young with a need to know;
    to trace shapes of healing
        plants in the dirt;
    later called foxglove, fennel, sassafras
    and goosefoot;
    their magic held in a pouch, to use with
        deft fingers,
          touch.
a quick body steps in haunting dances,
        sounds and yells push upward.
          bodies begin to sway.

to walk beside him listening, gave flight
    to feelings and thoughts.

the platform was dark against a dove colored
    evening sky,
        from high poles
the flutterings of banners flowed as part of the wind;
            stories left on air.

BRUCE EMBREE/INKOM

American Hero

Jeany and I went out to dinner last night
the food was good
We overheard a man who had really been up against it
and had somehow come out to the good

"The ball was almost completely covered in sand
but I played a wedge and came out
six feet from the pin"
He slouched back in his chair like the old vet
recalling the Jap machine gun he took out

   I was splitting firewood this morning
when Brigham the pup got run over
He just looked at me with his busted jaw
eyes already going funny
The animal doctor
will call if he don't come out of shock

   The mad old ayatollah
sends kids up against mines and tanks

   The silent millions die
cutting timber, digging ditches in Siberia

   You can drive along the freeway in El Paso
look across the border to shacktown
where kids die for lack of water
in the hundred degree sun

   These kinds of bad movies
are without end
list goes on and on
but don't you think there is something magnificent
uniquely American
Yes in a man standing alone
against it all
with his sand wedge?

April 25

   Road is full of holes I try to miss
on the way to Inkom or Pocatello
Water is almost over the road as the sun goes down
and has dropped three feet by morning
coming up a little higher every afternoon

> Geese and ducks, even storks and cranes
> are nesting or just hanging out
> down on the river or Marsh Creek
> Deer that lived have walked back up high
> later this year
> the snow was up to the top wire
>
> The Mormons are tilling their gardens
> plowing fields with tractors big as a bank
> Calves are born before the grass
> Hay trucks make two trips a day
> How can the snow pile up when it's going sideways
> instead of down?
>
> We get up at 6:30 in the morning and drink coffee
> then she goes to work and I fumble around for eight hours
> at times accomplishing little
> She gets home and we fix dinner
> lay around until eleven
> This seems right
> and requires no silly questions.

JACK FLEMING/OROFINO

Among Old Dancers

> The music comes brightly
> Into our lives.
> Close and tight he fiddles
> And the sweet, frayed notes
>
> Of "Red Wing, pretty Red Wing,"
> Are bowed off the strings.
> Waiting a turn, the others
> Bow or strum or pluck or tap.
>
> The dancers pump their arms
> To a variety of times;
> Old legs carry old bodies
> Across the measuring floor.

The music does not promise
A future or celebrate
A past but scatters around
Fragments of other times.

And pleases now what once
Glanced brightly from each eye.

Upon Hearing of the Death of a Boyhood Friend
Mooseheart, Illinois

It was not this world, the rotunda:
There was dancing to music that had taken
Years to shine past pillar and shrub.
A late spring evening and lightning bugs
Comforted the darkness, and do now that
Fifty years have come down on the dancers,
Fifty on the children who watched
And who imagined themselves four and five
Years later dancing around the rotunda
On their last spring evening—seniors, then,
On a world's edge that in a few days
They would disappear over. All did disappear.

Today that place and that time rise
Against other places and other times,
But more faintly, more faintly now,
And nearly without substance. The children,
Past childhood, one by one, yield to silence
And the dark. The rotunda, with its lanterns
And its too sweet music and its embracing
Dancers, recedes at the speed of life.

TINA FORIYES/MOSCOW

When in Drought

That summer she could not guess at goodness
and be surprised. Driving out of it,

she would always remain unsure
of the year, of the day of week,
of the specific unhappiness.

Her reality was emotion; her calendar,
the seasons. Abstinence and lack of rain
had centered her in thirst.

Hoping that motion and change would be solution,
she drove south to Grangeville,
consciousness closing on the heat gauge
and the plowed-under fields
where, right and left, smoke rose from the dirt
as though from secret fire.

Sun simmered from the open metal of the jeep,
cupped from the sky,
and she did not need a mirror
to see that she was burning.

It was after 3—in a landscape with no more shade
than the penciled shadow of a fence post—
that she came upon the farmer's homescrawled billboard,
"Praise the Lord, anyway"
and she parked in the comfort of its words.

Cabin Note

Have I forgotten to mention
the icicles?
        From the first flame of the fireplace
they began their bright growth,
glinting the eaves with no more brightness
than the high, cold stars.

        On the tenth morning,
looking back at the cabin from the riverbank,
they appeared to tusk the window.

From then on, I wrote from the throat of winter.

from *Jade Ring*

In the deep snow, spokes radiate from the cabin,
a pattern of need and desire,
indistinguishable as water and fire,
a fox and goose game
for one,

the mandala you follow to the woodshed,
where wind sluices white through dark slots
to lay snow slats in ghost fence
across the earth floor.

Halved wood, like cords of ideas,
rises to the rafters,
a mountain housed in darkness
and the scent of trapped sunlight.

An angry squirrel chitters the air,
and you fumble a barter of peanuts from your pocket,
apology and trust
against the emptiness of taking.

The cache of fur and cones you uncovered
the first week. Paused,
long enough among the tick of drying wood,
to recognize another's keep,
to hear toenail's tighten on the bark,
before the log was gentled back in place.

Now scolding is ritual,
and part of remembering a small, carved-wood box
and three kept-pieces of a jade ring,

as though time could bring it round again.

You kneel to the last carry,
and between the shed
and the gather at the cabin,
the trail is all breath and sweat,
until the woodbox lid drops,

and you hear the sound something makes
closing on itself.

Snowman in Summer

When I was first rolled into existence,
round head set on larger round of body,
the tallest boy's thumb printed the pockets
into which he pressed my marble eyes
and the pale girl screwed my carrot nose
into the center of its cliched face;
I did not know I had begun to be.

Upright,
in the cold silence of a yard,
I was a monument to a child's love of winter;
mentality no more than the loose drifting snow
huddled about my base.

Later, she came with book, across
pock-marked snow, and I felt her warm
and naked hands fashion lop-sided ears.
The first sound I heard was her voice
reading, "One must have a mind of winter
. . . and have been cold a long time . . ."

I learned a mouthless hunger
from her lips, "not to think of any misery
in the sound of the wind . . . ," and felt
the love in her thaw my round cold into desire.

"It's a poem," she said, "about you.
Mr. Stevens wrote it." And she touched my shoulder
with her soft "Goodnight." Then I began,
gift of her love: my virgin desire for life.

That first of nights awake
to the loneliness of her retreating steps,
the stiff slam of a distant door,
I ached a footless lust to follow.
Her voice beat will into my being,
"One must have a mind of winter . . ."
I could utter no call to stay her;
mouthless, my head bulged with words.

No syllable sounded in a throat of blood-flesh, no
trembling vocal cords, no lips to form the letters,
I stood as shaped silence and listened
to the cedar limbs fight chains of ice,
knowing their frozen pain for movement
as my own.

My marble eyes saw crystal beauty
and the warm gold square where she, pajama-bright,
cracked her window to call a second "Goodnight"
out to the darkness and me. Love burned my body
though winter I was. Had I arms
I would have held her startled vision
with a gesture of life, of gratitude
for love.

All night and the next day
at the iron hands of January winds,
in the heatless sun of dull winter skies,
I came to understand the words. I
who had no memory or fear of summer,
loved life and her with winter purity.
With February, a fierce thought of death,
and I learned from its alien cold;
though I was cold itself. And when my frame
shrank from strangely closer sun, I oathed
I would pass beyond my environment; not those
elements alone created me, but love,
her love.

I willed I would be a snowman
in summer for her, despite sun and sprouting
grass. Yet already, my marble eyes saw the line
of brown shag emerging in the sunniest corner
of the yard. I refused to look again,
though I knew it neared.

Finally, the weight of sun visions, magnified
by my glass eye, burned into the sockets
and the marbles dropped like rocks—
leaving hollow blindness,
I was without regret.

"One must have a mind of winter . . ."
and I imagined anew my first night.

Sight was no loss. Discolored
and rotted, my nose persisted as part of me,
though I could hardly suffer its presence
through which I smelled the stench
of itself. Irony was the knowledge
learned from my eyes; once the nose
would fall I would lose both
the recognition and the problem.
Still words held my being;
"One must have a mind of winter . . ."

I would return, for love of her,
a snowman in summer. Yet how small
the body becomes. I can no longer
hear or see. But love is the belief
I will be a snowman in summer for her,
I will be a snowman in summer . . .

JANE FRITZ/SANDPOINT

I Like Living Alone

As the moon seeps
through furrowed clouds
framing that old world.
Loneliness.
I would properly escape
if his charger strode up
nostrils breathing
red-hot steaming rescue.

The seduction scene
fascinates me.
Frailty and reluctance.
Hankering above imagination
as the moon draws a breath
at such a lie.

JANNE GOLDBECK/POCATELLO

Lava I

Even earth mutters in its sleep
as old dogs do,
and in their burrows, rabbits
twitch. A tremor
ripples through their nerves
out of the soil;
the same uneasiness threw mountains
to the north and south.
So many times a rift has split
the earthquake spine,
a burning habit rips old wounds
easily, viscid, slow-clotting.
Chronic eruptions that will not let
the old bones lie
rattle them down to slag and schist
until they rise
again.

Lava II

Volcanic crows
explode from the elms
like revelation,
raucous mix of wing and beak
under the crust of night,
beating its way to morning.
Some buried flames still
split the earth from time to
time, fountaining liquid rock,
dark blood from earth's
impatient veins,
tongues of lava sizzling in the dirt.
A deep, convulsive lightning
shakes the faulted,
pentecostal stone.

Winter Song

This month of sharpest stars, bitter, blue/white,
when starlike frost hangs in the lambent air
and cuts the lungs, as breathing splintered light,
can no warm gold domestic fires compare
with platinum, wildfire, January's flame
kindled from depths of ice by diamond sun.
Quick storms, awakened from deep solstice night,
fly crystal through the darkened trees, a rare
wild discipline of wings, whose glowing flight
leaves branches with new listening poise. They flare
frostsilver against dark, as cedars frame
bright waxwings' blaze, citrine and cinnamon.
Whatever grows burns with more vivid power
now in its wintering root than in its flower.

CAROLYN GRAVELLE/JULIAETTA

Is the Garden Worth It?

She fits into his life
like the worn-out heel
on his cowboy boot.
She rises for the ritual
fire at the woodstove
by four a.m.

Fields of discontent
range closely
but loudly
she jangles rosaries
recites novenas
counts:
      thirty-three quarts of green beans
      twenty-four rows of sweet corn
      twelve Jesus, Mary, and Joseph's
      potatoes three bags full
      and one red petunia plant
      by the back screen door.

Cooking blanches her appetite;
soaking breakfast plates drown
in dishwater bubbles.
Children sour her mind;
clothesline diapers wave
seven dozen surrenders:
she prays to St. Jude.

The dust stirs
with his entrance
then settles by her Daily Missal.
In bed
still worn-out
she devoutly
tends his evening chill.

FLORENCE GREATHOUSE/MOSCOW

Jackal in Red Stone

You've probably seen one yourself—
a scarab from Egypt. In the afterworld
the scarab protects our souls.

I wore the amulet one evening,
a carnelian with intaglio, gift of my mother,
and returning late, dizzy from champagne,
unclasped it carelessly. As the scarab
slipped off its chain, I heard no sound,
no conjunction of stone with tile, no
reverberation of matter with matter.

Its loss meant only the loss of an ornament
although my mother had spoken often
of its antiquity, believing I would in time
come to value the stone, acquiesce to its truth.

One night I was startled by a strong odor
of skunk. The dark room screamed until
I sat up, fully awake. The presence
filling me was gone by daybreak.

Now the scarab comes to me in dreams.
No longer encased in gold, it floats
in a vacuum. I can even see toothmarks
of the jackal who bites the stone,
and the stone bleeding its fine, red-orange
particles into dust devils. But these too
vanish as the scarab gyrates in its tomb.

I tell you this because the hieroglyph
does not lie, lies no more than our dreams.

Ghost Horses

That time we hunkered down
at the Moscow Mall waiting
for the famous Clydesdales,
they'd come to sell beer
but what they really sold
was horse flesh.
I watched people watch the horses,
strapping horses, solid as boxcars,
feet the size of skillets.
Some people looked into their eyes,
others wanted to stroke
their massive flanks. All the time
the horses stood silent,
occasionally twitching a tail,
shifting feet. No snorting,
bad temper, just resignation
bred into bone, centuries
of standing behind the plough,
of wrenching a war chariot
from foot-deep ruts in Etruria.
Then their trainers climbed
into the beer wagon, setting
the reins in motion.
The horses circled the Mall
before heading down Blaine Street.
A few kids followed the steady
clomp clomp of their hooves
on bicycles.

GERALD GRIMMETT/IDAHO CITY

Squeeze Play

The antelope
Had a blue eye.

I cross-haired the scope
Across 300 yards of sagebrush
And his eye came closer, blue,
Magnified through heat waves.

I slowly exhaled, and held.
The sun prismed like light
Through a bead of water.
His eye slowly turned brown
The color of wet earth.

CHUCK GUILFORD/BOISE

Maybe the Sky

Maybe the sky's a washed out gray and the stones
you've been counting on get lost, the simple fact
that you were born at all could make you act
the fool's part gladly when your frozen bones
go stiff and the only sound around's the slow moan
your mouth makes, the only sight the cracked
glass pane you never fixed, the frozen tract
behind it—waste, just waste. Look how you've grown.

Look how you've learned to turn away despair.
And though you can't quite find the way you came,
can't quite retrace those steps, can't quite say where
it is you're going, still it needs no name:
you've learned to carry silence like a prayer
so true it feeds you. No blame—no, no blame.

DEWEY HAEDER/GRANGEVILLE

Love Song in .20 Gauge

Chukar song, cross-canyon in the rocks
    an easy walk but for erosion's work
And I climb, obedient as hound,
    setting legs and lungs afire in those
        exquisite twin pains of lactic acid
    and no air

To the top, to
    Where They Were,
To where dog, nose awash in the
    molecules of their passing, says
    They Still Are.
I follow, trusting him
    and his compelling, dancing stub,
Until both lock up aquiver at the edge
    and I believe again.

It's this dance we come back for,
    meeting each fall in estrual rendezvous
You of the barred feathers and
        spring-steel legs,
I in Vibrams and .20 gauge,
    barrel hot and lusty,
        full of rut heat.
Joined, we hold in celebration,
    daring no movement
Until we all can wait no longer
    and I say Get 'em and he does.

You eject as one,
    diving
      accelerating
        downhill
then borne screaming   back up
    on electric pinions
To the crest, to that wild,
    lightning-struck, heaving crest
fuse with

The shots, convulsive,
    irresistible as flood,
Sending an ounce of gray passion
    to short-circuit winter's duty
Aim, lead, fire. A second time,
    a third
The hulls' metallic feeding quick as thought

Until a final time, when the action locks open
    and you are gone
        and we are left to crickets
            and the respirations of the canyon,

a feather floating in the updraft

SHARON T. HAYS/KIMBERLY

Success

a place in the country
where a horseshoe drive
half-circles a hedge
of peacocktails
Scotch on the rocks
is happy hour in poker face
too smart to smile
Inside a curved stairway
of polished bones where
your sullen mistress slinks
up and down a bad dream in drag
On the wall your soul
tanned taut and certified

Left

The knuckles I knock with
fall into nothing but hand
find a room full of your absence
your empty nap on the couch
silk of your sleep
still weaving the air

your name sprawls like catnaps
in the places you pressed your body
books tumble open-faced
where your eyes pulled words
off the page
packed them
into wrinkly gray luggage
and left
no forwarding address
nowhere to mail
the you-shaped hole in me
time to board up the doors
that only close

Skipping Rope in Hayden Lake, Idaho

Hardhat brickbat
Caterwauling thunder

Burn a cross total loss
Denigration plunder

Jesus christ miami vice
Abomination blunder

Pass the plate collect the hate
Put us six feet under

(turning faster)

Jesus hates us this we know
'cause the Butler told us so
off-colored skin is such a sin
Heaven is in Idaho
(faster)
Heaven is in Idaho
Heaven is in IdahoIdahoIdahoIdahoIdahoIdaho
(faster and faster until jumper trips)

BORG HENDRICKSON/KOOSKIA

Pam

Eighteen, eighteen,
A boogie to the slush of ice.
Swirls on the dance floor
And whirls in her mind,
She sang.
She sang songs of her childhood,
Of McDonald and his farm
While Pam and her lamb
Swaggered to the Ford.
Laughing, they say, and waving
Out the window,
She was gone.
Swerving at corners
That smiled calmly at the moon
Above green Daiquiri pastures,
She sped by.
She toodle-ooed "yahoo"
At the trudging of the tractor,
An orange spray of flowers
Of black rubber wheels.
The Ford leaped sideways
Across frozen timeways
Sprouting from the frost
In the field.
Crunched inside its cavern
Her body gaped forward
While her head gawked behind
Towards the route
From which she'd climbed.

JAMES HEPWORTH/LEWISTON

Silence as a Method of Birth Control

in some country of mountains
and woods that are tragic
because I say they are,
beyond my bootlegged dreams

of rivers and waterfalls,
canyons and thunder,
under the net of silver beads
some men call the sky,
who I am still awaits me.

Who I am still awaits me
though I certainly know
who I was: a black-bearded drunk
wading the blonde, dry-grass
of steep hillsides; bathtub fisherman;
lecher; vagabond; scholar; fool—
nothing, it seems, for which
I was wholly unsuited—
though when I do find myself—
as in the end I assure you
I will—

whether in the form of a snake
or the taut skin of a drum—
I wish to shake
all unawakened love
in the world and make
such a shocking, sexual hullabaloo
of our language merely to speak
will be considered an act
of conception.

Autumn in Inchelium

Autumn is cold in Inchelium.
Dark comes early, and although
I do not know the name for the season
in Salish, still, it is pleasant
to walk by the Trading Post
just as the electric lights come on
and to stare inside the huge windows.

Elsewhere, carcasses hang from pouches—
snow powdered thick in the fur
of the mule deer. Somewhere far away,
a phonograph plays a love song.

Each night the moon and I hunt this field
and fall in love with the earth.

Nobody enjoys the assassination
more than the hired killer. If you
should find me bent over books
inside my window, do not be mistaken:
I'm not always looking for ways
to impart the works of men. Most often
I search for a means to destroy them.

ED HUGHES/WORLEY

Settlement

Bought a glance
of canyon, quiet
creek cut, from rocky
mountain foothills
edging into lakeshore cattail bogs.
Could see the wind
divide the aspen,
spill the apples, sail
pine grosbeaks over branches
onto snowfields apple-brown
already deer-trail fixed.

Bought a feeling
wasn't thinking what
I spent so long to buy
the meadow voles had owned
as long as marsh hawks
had loved the seed-fat families
with flesh harvests,
oiling feathers and planting bones,
growing camas and vole spaces
in the process
that began before dollars
let people of vision
settle
for view.

Donnell Hunter/Rexburg

Otto

Now that Otto's buried we have
no one left to hate. He was meaner
than the rest of us combined.
He shot stray dogs, even those
that hadn't strayed, dragging
their bodies just across the line:
NO TRESPASSING THIS MEANS YOU!
He starved his horses till they girdled
all the elms. The County told him
cut them down before they fall.
He swore, fumed, cranked his chain
saw up at 3 a.m. and woke the town.

There was a woman once, but she
ran off, someone said. Maybe Otto
killed her. No one knew for sure.
Besides, who'd risk his wrath and turn
him in? It was easier hating.
No matter how mean we might become
he stayed meaner. It made us feel good.

But it's harder now. Dogs run wild,
kill sheep and chickens.

We have only ourselves to blame.

Louise

My life turned arty right after Louise
began to sing, her magnificent eyes huge behind
thick lenses that kept her from going blind.

It was a sound I never heard in our town,
one I knew would drive dogs wild.
I fell in love with Victor Herbert
and with Louise, though I was just a child.

At home I ripped out paintings from old
issues of *Life* Grandma handed down, hid
them in haystack tunnels sparrows made.

If you were quick, you could catch
a sparrow in your hand, feel its heart beating
like wings, like my heart in church
that night Louise began to sing.

For a dime I bought a book of poems
at the thrift shop, recited lines to cows, imagining
I was old enough to court Louise, listening

in her parlor as she, still a spinster,
sings Victor Herbert and my heart beats faster.

A Letter

If I wrote this from the dead
you wouldn't believe me. It's a good
wind that blows no ill. Best
to say things now. Whatever leaf
my life has turned, not every tree
has been a friend. I'd rather walk
on grass than concrete, take a chance
to trip against the stone.

So much for the salutation.
As for the body, I'll keep mine,
thank you, even though it may
betray me in the end. Each scar
adds up, each grain of sand.
Remember the year of the limp?
Now every step's a blessing,
no matter how far, how long I run.

When I write, I want birds
to listen, clouds to forget to hide
the sun. But to tell the truth
there's not much to tell.
My sins were not all that scarlet.
However dark the night, know this:
I never found another lover,
never needed another friend.

RANDY HUNTSBERRY/MOSCOW

Tripwire

> . . . the very dust upon which you now stand
> responds more lovingly to footsteps [of my people]
> than to yours, because it is rich with the blood of
> our ancestors and our feet are conscious of
> sympathic touch.
> Chief Seattle

The end of the war never ends.
Hundreds hide out in Olympian rain forests
behind hedgerows of scotch broom
bright yellow Iceland poppies
and blackened tripwire
thin as fish line
crisscrossing mossy perimeters
early warning those who remember
no comrade's name in the dim light
of beer bottle lanterns
full of bear fat.
They squint forever
from the end of the war
over homemade Claymore mines
big as manhole covers
over clear fields of fire
covered with purple lupine
anxious to kill
encroachers who come too close
in the night as they listen
to their own ears.
Mornings they poach game
pick fiddlehead ferns and polypores
pile beer cans beside their shacks
like crumpled bones, crouch
ready to spring
at any sign of life.

BILL JOHNSON/LEWISTON

Moose

You—
plunging your ponderous prow
through carpets of duckweed
and bluegreen algae
on this quiet lake, are you so
blind you don't see me
lurking by this drift-log,
stalking your face?
You—the gargoyled paragon
of gnome, smooching a world
of water and moss,
your snout a pendulous lobe
of pry, weighted
with great bone flagons,
your eyes surprisingly tiny, near-
sighted, as if you saw
always at a hazy distance, the light
just-dusk, your snout
a taproot sucking it out
again. Now you catch my drift
and lumber off through thick brush
never far from water,
the massive hinges of your shoulders
banked on a delicate heart.

Wildrose Cemetery

I stop to stare at the way
wind carries the snow over fields
bared by the plow.
I hear it jangle the flagpole
by the small church, closed and cold.

In the sanctuary, a row of paint-chipped pews
and an old piano with one good key,
brittle, but clear. Outside
markers tinged with lichen and moss.
Hard work and prayer have come here

for their final test. And maybe just once
(you go by hints, a rustle,
something in the air) a mother knelt
by a stone and prayed.
Someone breathed close, and was gone.

Someone remembered only in the mark
of a chisel, that cold refrain.
The stone is hidden by a pale green vine,
a rose, all I can see
of her name.

> *for daughters they lost*

ROBERT JOHNSON/LEWISTON

Your Mother's Story

After looking all day we arrive at the one house
I can afford: two small shells pushed together
like a *T*, a sad shingle roof and chalky paint,
foundation of rock given to lean. It is a shape
I can't name, until you call out from the doorway
line shack, hauled here from the woods
like a last load of logs.

                    I watch your hands
move across the rough boards, push the door tight
against some remembered wind, and you tell me
your mother's story, how she searched for houses
in the logging towns where she lived, finding those
she could reclaim from despair, the rent
paid with work, door frames reset
and shimmed with the heart of cast-off wood.

It was what she learned in that land,
how to work hard as any gyppo
when rain comes and the slick woods claim
a neighbor. Each time the same:
every man's eyes gray as sky,
not daring to look at his wife or the widow
shrouded in her new life, and in that room

only the stove made noise, a low pop and creak
like a tree spinning off the stump.

It was a sound she knew, a warning
stronger than any bell, and its echo
followed her, one house traded for another,
a new town, each job a measure of survival.
That day in November, a storm tore limbs
from trees, widow-makers' spike tops
whipped the sky, and rain rattled the roof
like gunfire. Behind her, the stove creaking
its loudest, she did not hear the radio, *Kennedy*,
or *Dallas*, but believed the neighbor ran for her, ran
the long road between houses for one reason.
She cried then for another wife, a small boy
mourning his father, cried harder still for the voice
she half-heard saying *thank you, thank you.*

And then silence, the move to the city
where I met you and where we stand at its edge
and the beginning of trees. What would your mother say
to this house, this life? Your hands are red with paint
weather can't erase, and creased with lives other than your
    own,
a line smooth and clear as cedar, a hard straight grain.

DARYL E. JONES/BOISE

Un Bel Di

I was turning to tell you something, I don't recall what.

On the far side of the lake it was evening already,
    the mountainside gone dark,
and along the public campground at the shoreline,
    the first supper fires
lifting a thin blue haze above the trees.

But where we were sitting the light was all around us,
    still going down gold, touching everything
as if it might never return—

                                        and I was going
            to tell you something . . .
                                    Then someone on the other side

    of the lake turned on a tapedeck or radio, the volume
            all the way up . . .
                                    And suddenly
    there was nothing to say that wasn't implicit already
            in the gold light leaving everything
    and that clear soprano voice, thin with longing,

    coming to us from a long way off, across water.

Maidenhair

Look, I hear you say, *how delicate.*
And stopping, turning around

under a rain-bright canopy
of second-growth spruce and fir,

I think how easily it might
not have been: this moment

shimmering in returning light
after a summer shower, this hush

on the forest floor, steaming
and fragrant. But no, you are pointing

over there, to a clear-cut stump
healed-over by lichen and moss,

where a clump of maidenhair
has randomly taken hold, and

sending its taproot
deep into heartwood,

lifted a delicate tracery
into the chartreuse light,

its slender fronds unfurling,
curling through one another, like

your fingers, now, through mine.

JOAN JUSKIE-NELLIS/IDAHO FALLS

Lee Driving through Colorado

His eyes pull him up canyons,
drag him into rivers,
sweep him into sky,
follow a flying hawk

Always this search
to the edge of the road,
then back, a little straighter
into the curve.

Over the next
mountain, deep within canyons,
two elk feed below the moon
we cannot see.

LINDA KITTELL/TROY

Island Leaving

When the last bits
of camphor-yellow ice
leave the shore, the island
re-collects its dead.
The spring earth breaks
under Oscar LaBombard's backhoe. The graves
line up. All the while
the first graders
chant the passing of time—days
of the week, months
of the year, small mouths chattering
a ritual of seasons. We
scour the shore

for our losses: the three
French nuns who visited the Shrine
turn up on the Alburgh Tongue, splinters
of oar and rowboat tight
in their fists, bits of toes, parts
of fingers missing, delicately chewed
we think. We find
the Lockerby shanty. My brother
is afraid we'll find Earl
face-up, fish-eaten.
But there
are only remnants of him—bits
of yellow flannel, a bright lure,
fish heads—the usual debris
that lines our shores.
How is it
that what the dead leave
takes on such importance? A tin bailer can, one
sneaker, five feet
of anchor rope are usually not
such treasures.
If Earl
Lockerby is found,
it will be after
he's traveled some distance, after
he's seen enough.
It's one way
to leave this island, to leave
the clutter of our lives together, the clutter
of Mondays
that pass on to Tuesdays, of summers
into falls
when poplars dabble
the lake with yellow leaves
and larch needles
lap against the shore
like bits of ice.

Rhonda LaBombard

First the Carlson kid, Charlie Ames and Harley Jarvis,
even Peanut Lockerby, and Earl—

I have tried to forget
everything I know about love, that town
west of here that pulls me back.
The courthouse deserved a clock. Johnson Avenue,
the main street, held seven bars, the Jet Club and Una's.
Expensive White boots and friscos, beer and Skoal,
red plaid elbows at right angles. I called him Cowboy
and he called me Girl, wiping
his glasses clean often enough
for me to remember. We danced across
sawdust, around folding chairs
until we were miles apart. I think
they tore down the Lumberman's
this winter. I think
the police chief and his whorehouse
are dead. Nothing really matters, that distance.
Some days, I could put on my best dress
and drive across Kansas singing
Johnny Rodriguez. Some days, I could leave here
in a minute. Some days,
he was that kind.

ALEX KUO/MOSCOW

The River

We live by it, bank deep
By choice near where some ducks
Have also come to believe
This fierce geography that the wind
Will not forget in the next change.

We live in it, in its echo
That is a question, and what it asks
Is a breath forming its words
There on the opposite century, here
On this seamless shore, this abundance.

One year I followed it back
To its beginning in a glacial gap
The next night all the seasons moved
A half moon over my head rising
At last released from all counting.

We live by it, in its story
Dispersed as we are flesh in its eddies
Of meaning, this wider water
And its settlement among leaves
Glittering with teeming assertion.

We live like this, our breath
Over the river's edge, reason
Collecting at the changing waterline
Where only a vague mark forms
Between promise and possibility.

A Chinaman's Chance
Shanghai, 1945

When the bombs dropped on us at the end of the war
no one knew which side did it. We were under
Blankets, beds, that inside table, even chairs

Later when I walked out of the dropzone, I counted
The steps that were not mapped at the beginning
Wanting everyone to have the same, necessary things

Hundreds were queued up on every street corner
For airdropped powdered milk, chocolate, condoms
By the same planes that dropped the bombs the night
before

If the truth be known, I had to kill to get away
Lucky, as luck would have it, I wasn't born
In the 18th century: Mozart loved slurs then

For heroes now, I retain Clemente, Gould, my two sons
And what the wind leaves: they have been here
All this time nearer my life, nearer my starfield

For direction, I call on the far points
That insist at intervals without explanation
That left me in the last, unmarked C-46

Like that last flight out of Casablanca in 1940
In the fog and at gunpoint, just like that
Shutting out of a life, leaping past the finish

Do not mistake me or look for me in another meaning
Where I won't be found. In a sense we have all survived
Our words depend on it, with each chance

CAROL JEAN LOGUE/SPIRIT LAKE

Cornucopia

You play the guitar
while I marvel at color
of cranberries, glossy with
honey, the cup, extra half
of pecans and almonds,
orange peel, juice, flour
to bind into loaves.

You finger the chords
simple, sweet, sour and draw me
from bowls to your memory of
other chinooks, warm glossy
winds melting snow, flashing
rain in December.
Winter boy who was bad

and had to stay in after
school every night until white
revealed green, a season
away by anyone's guess;
a chinook intervened and
melted it all in a day.
I say I could write

your stories to poems
for the rest of our lives.
Lights flicker. You yawn.
The wind moans, croons, intones,
sweeps her skirts among trees
as I bake the bread
and you strum pandora.

All-giver from honey vase
whirling and whistling
weaving and wild

pouring blessings and curses
in every affliction
in birth, death, rebirth
in hope as we stir by the fire.

You lay her astride
and head up to bed
while I long in the dark
listening, I listen to
song in the rafters
watch moon dance and laugh
wait till sweet sour sacrament cools.

STEPHEN LYONS/MOSCOW

Women Out West

When women go mad out West
you find the bottles
behind the dryer.
Trails of sadness first detected
as fatigue, discovered as madness.
        You think it must be you. But then.
Stale breath and clenched words, bumping into the
refrigerator, falling asleep in the middle
of dinner.
You tell the children she's tired.
But they know.
You don't.

When women go mad out West
checks bounce.
Car breaks down, dogs
starve and lunge tied to fence posts,
grass burns yellow, weeds snake through broken
windshields.
        This can't be happening. Again.
At dawn.
When only you get up
and notice her next to you.
Fully-clothed. In shoes with knots you cut.
She calls a name,
not yours.

When women go mad out West
seasons blur.
Bulbs never surface.
The north walks stay icy in May.
Windows won't budge, long ago sealed in latex.
    Everyone knows. About this.
And yet.
You can only tell her she really was young before this
town
with the rotting grain elevators.
And combines that swing down Main about August.
When heat rises off the barley to shake cottonwoods
and home seems to leave with the chaff.

House of Wind
for Dick Hugo

When you come West,
come with momentum.
Bags packed, good car
and back-up cash.
You will come a stranger.
Good houses with nice porches
window-boxes and a view.
People you will never be.

Seek no fortunes here.
Long ago locked up in
pits, clear-cuts and hydro-madness.
Those who came first.
Boom, then always busted.
Those with bones earthed
below neon droppings.

Face crossroads of no horizons.
Choices run dry like
a house of wind.
Train stations scream for leavings.
Hollow pickup half immersed.
A time suspended road-kill.
Years pass only crowsfeet,
worn boots and the letters home.
Can't explain.

Pass here without notice.
That night with train whistles
and a light swinging shores
of the Yaak River.
To wake and count the white crosses
you finally become.
Like a trace of snow that
stayed too long.

LINDA MCANDREW/BOISE

Memoirs of an Idaho Falls Carrot Snapper

Her shoes are zippered and tagged
like corpses in plastic bags,
her blouses folded in tissue.
She does her best at first,
cracking derailment jokes as she backs
away. The other passengers bawl
and fill sandbags at seeing
a journey fall apart so soon.
She makes polite excuses—
bedbug bites, a sprained ankle—
but really it's the shoes,
the blouses and three dozen
moist towelettes.

When she climbs over the sandbags,
she's in a dusty hotel
near the station. She signs
the register and grabs her key,
relieved to be only halfway there.
Then, after she's had a swim
and a drink, after they've closed
the shutters, there's nothing to do
but lie naked on the bedspread
and surrender her skin
to the heat. What she needs
is buckets of rosewater
to rain down on her,
a shower of salamanders,
a miracle of nectar.

She needs someone to beat down
the door and read her her rights.

TOM McCLANAHAN/BOISE

Heartland

I drive into the heartland
Flanked by the spokes of fields
Turning beside me,
Inside me,
Adjusting to the speed of my recollection
Like a great earthen wheel
Spun from the energy of matter and desire.

Woods pass darkly.
Wind crackles through the corn, hums in the wheat.
A combine lumbers like a dream,
Its locust whir saturates the morning.

This far inland the soul flattens like the land,
Expands with the accumulating ghosts of machinery in
    barnyards.

I enter the heartland through the eternal August of women
Emerging from canning cellars, kitchens, gardens,
Smelling of grass, of growth,
Deep rooted in summer,
In patience.
My aunts are cats, milk drenched.
My sisters sprout like radishes.
And, deeper in the dark past,
Rooted agelessly in the yard,
My mother wraps a kerchief around her careless head.
In the heartland dream she absorbs us all again—
The farm, the heat, the goodness of memory—
And we are forever fat, forever fresh.

I see the men,
Pouched out, hands behind them, reeking of alfalfa,
The grease of machinery barns, the dust of auctions, of
    attics

And all manner of feed.
They survey their land,
Their brothers' land,
Their fathers' land,
And, again, their own.
It is a plain surveying, a counting up,
A late-summer reckoning of what was spent and what
    saved,
Of profit and loss.

I walk the precarious loft,
Testing the floor as if my caution in itself
Will lighten up the weight.
A senseless, sunlit shaft has crossed me,
Dissecting the dark intrigue of boyhood,
Illuminating the ancient tools—
A splitting wedge, the sharpening wheel,
The saws (worn through),
A wooden scythe,
The rusted rat trap, sprung.

I kick the granite wheel
Until its breathing hums along a blade.

Behind the barn I take a road leading nowhere
But not to its own beginning.
Not much more than a weedy path
(And these weeds fast becoming trees),
It starts from the top of the hill, wanders to the creek,
Crosses there to the lowland fields, then turns around,
Rejoining itself for the climb back up.

I sense the nervous cows, long dead.
I pass the old bridge, buckled.
The deserted hives,
The treehouse with its steps intact,
But all the floorboards rotted out,
The sunken tractor, the camping ground.

A combine lumbers through the wheat,
Its locust whir saturates the morning.

I finally find the well,
Water rising like language,

The ancient machinery still a mystery to me.
How were they sure of water here?
How did it stay repaired so long?
How is the water so precisely cool?

We honor private places, protect deserted things.
The wheel.
The woods.
The cellar.
The loft.
The combine.
The path.
The well.
All things have meaning in the heartland.

By the sagging gate of a broken farm,
Where the well water waits,
Where the slow sun descends,
I start the car.
I start the machinery of heart and of mind,
The engine of all things,
And, for a while, idling,
A great wheel turns again on its firm axis,
A human wheel,
Bearings greased but grinding
Like a metal blade on a granite disk
Through all my darkening doubt.

The Farm

At last, long last, the farm became too much to bear.

The domestic stock diminished with every season
As cultivated land gave way to wild growth.

And I too was diminished.
I too grew wild,
My thin hair bursting out of all control,
My wholly human tongue silenced by the slow, chaotic
    change.
I plodded with cows at auction,
Rode bleating with the sheep in rear ends of pickups,

Bled with the final ewe, chased down and tangled in
    barbed wire
Just twenty feet from a hole so wide
A combine could drive through.

With the cats that were not drowned
I wandered out of the corn crib and off to other farms,
Stealthily navigating the secondary roads.

With the lumbering sows I broke the pen,
Rutted out the vegetables,
And made short work of a new litter.

My neck cracked with the chickens and ducks
So surely ended in the dinner pot or frying pan.
Their aroma filled the house for days.

I stampeded with the ponies,
A shaggy, shadow herd roaming the lowlands by the creek
Or scattering in the corn-stubble fields.
We thinned with every winter,
Though our hair grew out like the manes of mythic beasts.
We haunted the place until we could run no more,
Our foundered hooves curling back on us.

One summer night
I awoke with the weight of the lone mare passing on my
    heart.
My haunches quivered shamelessly
Until she dropped of age in the stall.

That very week I heard the windmill squeal its last
With a gust of howling from the north.
It dropped, a skeletal dream across the garden.

Unleashed, I turned wolfen with the surviving dogs,
Yelping the hills in game pursuit of what then seemed
Like every living thing that moved.

I ran the darkened woods,
Howled at the waning moon,
Howled at the waxing moon,
Howled at the circling hawks
And the crows atop the cottonwoods.

Toward the very end I became the plants,
Curling inscrutably with the grapevines,
Going to seed with the final rows of cabbage, turnips,
    celery.

In the last aimless summer,
I left the house and slept outside,
Spreading out under stellar fires in universal dark.
I stretched out over every inch of measured space
The farm could claim.
And as the cheatgrass sprouted from my eyes,
As the creek burst from my chest,
As the fire of every living thing now dead or gone
Trembled like our common, savage self,
I raised a single cry above the house and barns,
Above the human graves,
Above the very dust,
A raging out of energy itself,
A ranting from my heartland's core,
A common vow for all of us to be remembered long,
But never to be tame again.

Ron McFarland/Moscow

Out Here

Even a stone can astonish us,
thrown or underfoot, rippling the surface
of some dark pond
or stumbling along in the dust
if we give it a chance.

In New York, L.A., Chicago, even Seattle
passions run riot in ways we cannot feel
with our stingy sensibilities.
People keep on living as if
they were going to die
in the next minute,
so of course they do.
A friend who works for the *Wall Street Journal*
says it's the only honest way to live.

Out here we live as if
we're going to live forever.
We spend carefully.
The Forest Service and the B.L.M.
send college students into the field
each summer to count sagebrush.
They are contemplating a program
to tabulate tumbleweed,
full employment year-round.
It's an education.

The friend from Manhattan
visits one of our short summers,
waiting daily for something to happen.
It never does. The whole summer
is like skipping stones
late in the afternoon on a placid pond.
We try to talk, but she's too deep,
like a stone seeking the bottom.
Out here we like those conversations
where no one has the last word.

Town Marshall

Small towns like this, mills belly-up
about like me, don't need but one cop.
Main thing is to know
everyone's business like your own.
I grew up in this town,
busted my back at the mill,
took over marshall when no one else
wanted it. I got divorced so fast
I almost didn't get married first.

Don't need no damn diploma
for this sorta work,
just common sense and knowing
when to grin, when to cut the bull.
Get along with the high school kids
you got it made.
I wink at six-packs
on the floor of the back seat,

but no drugs or hard stuff.
Dip a little snuff
with the old boys down at C.J.'s,
find out what's going on,
it's not a hard job.

Now this new council wants a cap and gown,
Police Academy instead of a badge and gun.
Thirty years, and now
some college kid in a coat and tie
tells me I can't run two miles
I ain't a good cop.
Hell, it's like I told the council,
this town don't need a good cop.

Orgy

Clicking and scraping, the buttons and zippers
awaken me from my drunken half-sleep.
Inside the dryer the clothes are throwing a real party,
an orgy of sleeves and half-slips, bras
tossed about like straws in a gale of lust,
jockey shorts clinging ecstatically to silken
bikini panties, my gray polyester dress slacks
clinging wantonly to some woman's silvery negligee.

My God, it's my wife! But what's a woman like her
doing in a place like this? The lewd heat, the cheap
perfume, the tawdry darkness in corners,
the monotonous rock and roll of a local group,
idle chatter, a storm of romantic boredom.
You call this an atmosphere for love?

Awake, my dove! Come out in your warm
wetness and cavort with me under the stars.
Let us reach overhead and pluck the strings
of the sky's violin. Let us dance all night
in the cool wind and waken at dawn refreshed,
side by side in the calm, dry certainty of ourselves.

A Perfect Day

Man, the blue sky yipes all day
like workshirts on their own time
playing a clumsy game of softball,
and the sun will not go down
without whistling or winking
at a lazy pop-fly the outfielder,
who played a little pro ball once,
is too kind to catch, and the wind
cooperates, and the rich grass
bends at the ankles, and the girls,
the women, the grandmothers bloom
among the dandelions and sweet clover,
all of them wonderfully inarticulate.

God, the meadowlarks pounce on the air
like brief interruptions and carry themselves
away, and the soft hoots of the owl
this morning prophesied their flight
along with the soar of the white ball
and the roar of the shortstop toppling
impossibly after it, and the women's
light laughter and teasing shower of
carefully gathered grass clippings that stick
to his sweat polished back, and still
the sky delights everyone with its intimations
of something beyond pure color,
and a pair of killdeer suddenly sing out,
surprised by evening.

ANNE MERKLEY/POCATELLO

Gold on Blue

We who turn dark faces
from purple shadows holding conversation with the
    ground,
running ahead of our steps
to melt a worm's way through the blades of grass
    expanding the edge of their own purple seas—

We who turn become
light-embossed silhouettes wearing crowns of hairwire
   touched by the fire
   of fingertip rays
      Walk our eyes up those rays
to a weary after-summer sun
dying with the year
      Wave farewell to
the wavering exit of whitehot
   crystalline rainbow presence
   spilling from its socket in over-the-hills western air.

   We who turn
in this turn of time
   hear closer our foetus-stirring hearts ask
      What do the leaves of this tree say
      Why their fragile tremble here
like a chill through the threadbare cost of a fading day?
   And in the October that they shed
   upon us with their fall

we who turn find ourselves broken at any wandering wrist
   that would thrust an explosion through
   any taut paperlike blue
      Become weak in the impatient will
that would impose a collapse on
   any redwhite yellow hour
   behind this moment
      this moving tree
   holding picture still

And the golden orange leaves
continue to dance on blue.

J. I. MILLS/IDAHO FALLS

Ascension

Behind his cabin is a garden with large
comfrey plants. At dusk the bees are gone.
The old man meets the young woman here.

He is teaching her what he learned in China
many years ago.
He shows her how to move her arms
like a crane spreads its wings.
The wings of birds, he tells her, are feathered
and filled with light stored in hollow bone;
they float through dark skies like eclipsed moons.
The secret, he tells her,
is to store light in your bones.

She believes him when she comes
to the garden one evening and finds him
collapsed about himself, dark and empty,
arms like a crane akimbo, mouth open
frozen on his final words: like a bird,
he tells her.

There is enough light, she says,
for all of us to store in our bones.
In the end it will float us off this earth.

ALAN MINSKOFF/BOISE

Pounding Nails

Think of him as house
bound with a hammer.

He commands the inside
terrain, twists a slow screw

driver, sets finish nails
in straight grains. His

trade is amber, slate or
mackerel skies. He pounds

10 penny nails and daydreams
in the Tetons, the Sawtooths

the Bitterroots, the Owyhees.
A man who deals in moons

and deserts not the money
market and tax frees.

He prefers memory to tv,
rivers to reservoirs, obscure

Rocky Mountain ghost towns
to Boise, Reno, or L.A.

Think of him as house
bound with a hammer

hands buried in sounds.

Idaho City

The gold helped fund the Union army.
Bigger than Portland for a time,
the frame buildings burnt like tooth
picks in sixty-five, again in
sixty-seven almost two years to
the May night. The old bricks
tourists see were constructed later
from local clay. The miners stayed
with the vein: it ran thin, they
moved like bees south to the Owyhees,
north to the Coeur d'Alenes. Reverend
Kingsley's ghost wanders Wallulah,
Main. He jabbers to anyone who
listens—what happens to men,
towns, for the love of ore.
Every building has a skeleton.
At the cemetery pines grow
through the graves.

ROB MOORE/TROY

Hometown Bar

In Troy there's a bar just like your house
only better: your wife's not there.

Long white curtains hang over the square
window like they did in the kitchen at home
those late nights after the baby slept
and your wife lay tossed in exhausted sheets
and you stayed awake, smoking, listening
to the radio's low drone and drinking
Jim Beam neat in a jelly glass, wood table
in front of you worn smooth as trouble by
the buffed fog of alcohol. Nobody bothers
to clean the ashtray. The door stays closed.
Women walking by on the street outside peek
over the curtain but they don't see you.
There's more whiskey than you can drink
in a lifetime, try as you might, in the clear
bottles stacked like cordwood against the cold.
The glass always holds enough oblivion
to drown in. Just like home.

Welcome Back

We never saw
those five mottled eggs
in the mud-daubed nest
crack and hatch, never saw
the fledglings, scrawny and love-
hungry, open their eyes in a blaze
of lilac. What a way
to begin life, crying
for food and mother inside
a palace of blossom, a Versailles
of soft lavender petal and pale yellow
center, repeated again and again until
tattooed in the sense it becomes
something other than self, something
other than blossom, some perception
that the whole world is entirely
beautiful and incredibly fragrant.
And what else is there? Moments when
we recognize the banked fire that holds
our world in its slow, sporadic boil, then
long stretches of time when we're away
from the burning bush, continuing

on faith, memory, a fragrance which
won't let us accept anything less.
Though we never saw them hatch, they did.
This year five new eggs ignite
in the ripe nest.

SHERYL NOETHE/SALMON

(untitled)

Yellow cars are
sliding sideways beneath the streetlight
and from all the rooms of my house
lurk dark looks.
Logs drop like footsteps in the stove and burn.
It's so cold that I know I am nude
atop a blue ball rolling headlong
into the illuminated void.

Ideas float from my head like a children's
illustration. I am afraid of many things,
living and dead, and I believe in hell.
So does the fourth grade.
They are afraid of their houses
and what a basement means at night.
I am riding earth into outer space
here on top of the world
which happens to be tonight.

JOY PASSANANTE/MOSCOW

Dream-Thief

Small daughter, while we still quivered, joined
in sleep, you, lodged deeper than any lover,
battered me awake
to each night train.

When finally I strained to free you,
you clung to that dark peace,
fought the chrome instruments,
my muscular thrusts, emerged

to a place blacker still.
Little hairs dark on shoulders and ears,
eyes circling wildly under thin lids, you were born
dreaming.

I know those dreams. While you crouched
in my womb, they fed on my memory,
traveled my blood.

You left my body
heaving for weeks, my tears sliding
along my face to your fists
that clutched and puckered my breast.

Now the same dark hair
falls down our necks
dark eye mirrors dark eye
in them the flicker of enemies.

Nights, you insist I look
into your room. When your eyes are closed,
I kiss them. Sometimes, in the thick
of midnight you stare at my picture
on your nightstand. Your cheeks
puff and suck, in and out, sheathing
your thumb. And still, lids open,
your eyes roll and dream.

When you refuse to sleep at all,
our voices climb, pitch for pitch.
Open-palmed and trembling,
I smack the wall. Your mouth stretches
in silence, as if
you have dreamed this before.

TIMOTHY PILGRIM/COEUR D'ALENE

Angle of Repose

It is only by degrees
we arrived by love's central core.
One by one, layered loam

scraped off bedrock
ready to support
some institution's graying weight,

we peeled lesser habits away.
Showering together was first to go—
your breasts streaking my chest,
mouth nuzzling lips,
spray erasing suds
I'd laid on your chin

with one bubbled stroke.
Late-night dinners went—
Bach swirling amid candled shadows,
your head snuggling in crook
of my neck and shoulder,
our humming moistened by chablis,

notes drifting mixed
amid concerto wafting upward
cooling in waxened smoke.
Sleepy hours together turned fetal,
became hug of knees—
no more pressing for warmth,

nose resting against back
as breath ebbed and flowed
in perfumed hair,
thighs molded to derriere:
Instead, one morning caress,
final layer removed,

yielding granite for our love
together. At last
we had a fine foundation to build on.

Pre-Dawn Vigil at Kootenai Medical Center

> "Son, thou art ever with me, and all that I have is
> thine."
> —Luke 15:31

My only boy lies unconscious,
tubes dripping hope back into cheeks

flushed ruby by I.V. flow. I see
last summer's campfire the two of us
blew to life in meadow dusk,
anglers' attempt to keep Montana cold

from freezing fingers off our fished-out hands.
This trip today, testing Priest Lake alone,
netted a limit of poison,
not nearly as much fun as bringing in
three Dolly Varden now untended,
glass-eyed beside the vacant boat.

I wish for Montana twilight, we two
shivering back the day's rainbows,
eager fighters jumping against the sky,
fierce competitors for royal coachmen
arced toward their stream—
invitation to exchange

icy creek for burlap creel.
Night flames took crackling hold
of lodge pole twigs gray with age.
I roughed his hair, brushed fire-red cheeks,
let loose laughter that followed ash
to coolness in the floating smoke.

His chest rises, then dives deep
in this struggle to keep life.
I hook his hand in mine,
catch and release with each faint breath.
At times I see sparks
sputtering against the night sky.

SCOTT PRESTON/KETCHUM

River by Picasso, 1903

You caught the river's winding
in a corner of your eye
and thought it was the figure
of a blue reclining woman.
As you quickly turned, she
disappeared

like all your new-found loves,
leaving your eyes with a curve of river
and fascination, old and still lost.

Another Story Sun Valley Never Hears

His father
was an old Scottish rancher
who ignored the doctor's order
of corrective lenses
for his son
as an unnecessarily expensive
extravagance
as the boy could still
herd sheep just fine.
Later, when Walt had lost
most of his eyesight
folks around town still remembered
he'd had a tough start,
helped refer him
to parking lot cleanups
and lawns to mow, even
got out of bed
when the bartender called
to drive him home
from the Silver Dollar
when he was too drunk
to make it on his own.
He used to grind an ancient
John Deere tractor
he'd inherited
to jobs
until the cops took it away.
Now he rides a careful Schwinn
on the righthand side
of the fading white line,
derelict saint
of the Hailey/Bellevue three mile
stretch, stoic steady pedaller
hauling a mower and gas
on a welding shop trailer,
bright orange warning signal flag
jerk-bobbing in the chainlink wind,

cigarette smoking the distance
like a star falling
from his lips.

STEVE PUGLISI/POCATELLO

The Arts in Idaho

> "Idaho is currently in last place behind all other
> states and six territories in funding which it receives
> from the state."
>
> *Idaho State Journal*, 9-7-84

Starvation, the crumbs from an unkept shelf,
A larder empty of all but promise,
The promise (and empty canvas itself)
Waits for its last supper, its judas' kiss.
Over a grave, poverty builds its house
On pairless two-by-twos and one-by-ones,
Barren winds dance through broken walls, rains dowse
The kilning fires, words spoil the set of suns.
Beyond valleys, mountains rise majestic,
Lure the eye and lull the mind, the land bathes
In dull moonlight while coyote songs stick
To the sky like frozen fur, no one stays.
Still, we fashion a life of sorts, a feast
Of dregs, play the beauty to pay the beast.

PENELOPE REEDY/FAIRFIELD

I Continue

planting cabbage,
moving strawberry plants
and watching cranes perform
            south of the house.

I continue
with my books and pens
like a mouse gnawing at a musty shelf
            of forgotten words.
My heart opens to dust.

I do nothing with great effort,
wondering at my regrets when I reach 80.

I continue to laugh
to feed chickens
and tie shoelaces.
I listen to the prairie wind
hoping for storms to ease my rage,
my silent rage,
my desire,
of the kind in books
that in my innocence, I never believed.

A pair of geese pass over.
One pair.

I turn to face the mirror.
Feathery brush strokes on my lips
conjure you up, that one kiss,
like no others.

When I can no longer endure the pain,
when it ceases to be sweet,
I will keep my lips bare,
colorless,
and turn my head at the sight
                of cranes dancing.

WILLIAM STUDEBAKER/TWIN FALLS

Where You could Live Forever

When they laid the track
through the high desert,
they didn't know
where this town would grow.
But like a bull-thistle
it sprang up in a little good dirt
just north of nowhere.
Its Main Street, cut in half
by the train track,
formed the only two streets.

Here dad strode into manhood,
staggered from Main to Main,
sometimes taking years
if he caught a train
on its way through.
Whenever he came back,
he jumped off
on the other side of the track,
landing on his feet, headed
the way he had been going.

As old as he is,
he still staggers
from Main to Main,
wondering what he will do:

time is what the train carries,
change is what Main Street
never made, and so few people
have died in this town,
they've lost the key
to the graveyard gate.

Sandpoint

Old lady Weil
came here rough as an Iowa cob,
but the years pushed against her like waves,
wearing her skin smooth as the beach
she hobbles down to town.

And old man Deshon
sits in his sixty-four Ford
counting his four missing fingers,
remembering when he
set chokers with one hand.

So many dreams have drowned
in this lake. . . .
The fish get bigger each year.
And tonight, a young logger
takes old lady Weil's granddaughter

out on the point,
holds her, raising his arm
with four good fingers
toward a fish rising
to swallow the white lure of the moon

knotted to a string
buoyed to the rest of their lives.

Jukebox Cave

On an abandoned Air Force base near Wendover, Utah

There is no music now
unless you count the elegy
limestone sings inside itself
or the hum a cave makes.
But if you had a megaphone
made of time
and turned it toward history,
you might hear Glenn Miller
some moonlit night. . . .
And you would be tempted
to pick a song on the jukebox
and sit wrapped around
a long-neck bottle of beer
and let the cool air
dance through your hair.
Another dozen beers
(who's counting the songs?)
and fatigue would open
like a parachute,
and you would, finally,
start coming down
on a beach water abandoned
thousands of years ago.
And nothing time could do
would push you from your chair:
so well-centered
the world would have to spin
around you.

Nowhere Near

This is the road to Bone.
Goes through Ozone.
Just Fletcher left
a seventy-year-old drunk.
But with enough water to hold
his own ground.
Says he's selected a grave site
big enough he won't
have to lock a brake
just to turn around.

Bone: good people making ends meet
as well as anybody nowhere.
But their rope's a hair short
just a bunch of has-beens
unraveled so long the twist's gone.

This is the road to Bone
lazy as a bullsnake
stretching its loins long
into the sunset.

Past Ozone. Just outside of Bone
there's a wind for which the nose
is untrained, a thin argument:
heatwaves, the beards of winter wheat
a ridge too sharp to define.

Fletcher says everything's
a matter of taste:
What the wind is. Why some folks
settle one problem with another.
And for as far as he can see
he's still nowhere near making it.

FORD SWETNAM/POCATELLO

One Winter

Snow on the mountain again;
Boot-deep and windblown,
It fills the north gullies
And fans onto the lee side
To slip down the alluvium
And briefly green the fields.

For the winter wheat,
It's Spring, but on the ridge
The wind tightens like a fretted string,
And darkness freezes in the draws all day.

Down low the river thickens.
Steam frosts the brittle willows.
Though there's good sun yet
And the air is still,
Cows clump where the hay will drop,
Horses turn from the remembered wind.

Another Winter

Tonight the snowline's down
To five thousand feet,
And on the benchland
The big flakes jitter
Between snow and rain
As speech jitters on skin
At the tip of the tongue;
It's another night when the borders move,
And the big flyways
Fill with the voice of geese;
Even the humans, heavy of blood,
Jitter and almost fly—

Birthday Metamorphoses

Gerald, this one makes forty;
Must be a long-handled spoon
You were born with,
And good luck in that charmbag
Near your thighbone.

Brother, we have known dry times
And times when if there had been water
We wouldn't have touched it,
And though we have dodged the taxi
That ran down Diamondfield Jack,
We'll never know the renewing trick
Of the Big Lost River;
A thousand springs but only one sink.
We have to live it here, and
Just living in dry country is
A full-time job; finding new water
When the earthquake shifts
The springs is harder still.

I hope your art will not wear out your body,
And that our backs and knees stay desert-wise.
Our livers we will sell to a retired couple
Who like to fix things up.

I doubt the old Fisher King
Will make his limit trying these muddlers
Again and again
                    but we'll hang on
Because sometimes even when evaporites
Ring the sinkhole like a scab there's water:

In Southeast Idaho, in August
The cumulus sits above the cottonwood
And rides its own draft to forty thousand feet,
Where it spreads like the hand of God
Letting a sinner through the cracks,
And with the tree exchanges rain.

Pioneer League, Butte vs. Pocatello

Fertilizer plants in their summer layoff
It's a high sky for the Dominican outfielders
Who must first pick the ball out of the sagebrush
On the eastern hills and then
Track it against the cumulus stack
Made by the same updrafts
That fade or slice the ball.
A few trains hump in the yards,
Kids shag fouls in the parking lot,
And a man in gold pants
Swings a metal detector above the gravel.

Then there's a ball in the gap
And the rightfielder with the good arm
Who is starting to hit gets there for it
And while the throw catches
Peach light on its way to the cutoff man
The three hundred fifty-one of us
Who sang the national anthem
Forget that the town is hitting .237;
We have another chance to catch the runner.

TOM TRUSKY/BOISE

FROM *Lewis & Clark Sequence*

Opulence

. . . *Sah-cah-gar-we-ah* or Indian woman was one of the
female prisoners taken at that time; tho' I cannot discover
that she shews any immotion of sorrow in recollecting this
event, or of joy in being again restored to her native
country; if she has enough to eat and a few trinkets to
wear I believe she would be perfectly content anywhere.

Merriwether Lewis

The opulence of memory.

Who amongst us
who can afford it
is blameless?

Only the brute or beaten?—
these starving dogs
ravenous for scraps
of mere day-to-day,
gristle and suet, bones and skin
thrown from tables
where a fondness for the past
and prime shanks
thrives.

Is it wonder,
as scars and calluses accumulate,
as belly bloats,
who turns childlike and mute?

They know the answer
is no answer.
They have put aside
hope,
the gew-gaw that it is.

Cataplasm

. . . At sometimes for a moment I thought it might be a
dream, but the prickley pears which pierced my feet
severely once in a while, particularly after it grew dark,
convinced me that I was really awake, and that it was
necessary to make the best of my way to camp.

Merriwether Lewis

. . . Marrowbones and trout,
hump of buffalo.
And recall
embers, stirred,
a flurry of orange moths
rising to the stars,
vanishing . . .

How else should we survive?
We, the fortunate, the doomed
who age,
who have pasts
with which we must come to live.

What would we have children relish
for their future,
as if children
had no lives
to live for
but the lives
from us
they learn.

Let us
with such poultice
staunch wounds
the world has waiting.

That these brevities of healing
be known by children
who, from their journey,
stagger into camp,
their eyes blanched
or burning.

EBERLE UMBACH/McCALL

Theatre in the Heartland

Morning grows back like the arm
of a starfish. The old woman
puts on a dress that's shiny
as a blue-bottle fly.
The trailer walls
are fiberglass—light comes
through the little veins.
Big veins pump underground
rippling up through the cornfields.

Crows land in the miniature yard;
the laundry is flapping.
Warm days they take baths
in the puddle. She folds her arms,
her chin tucks into her neck—
"They try everything," she thinks

"to get me to look."
They preen so they can stand
in the rain, tiny misshapen cows
that need milking.

She's not fooled. Just smiles—
presses fists to her mouth
laughing.
The crows start laughing too
taking beakfuls of sky.
She's afraid she'll get drunk
with so much happiness.

A Room in Idaho

My husband sings a German lullaby,
I count knotholes on the wall—
none are missing. The window presses
its quiet thumbprint through my body—
barbed wire the nearest horizon,
foothills trailing off into yellow rhymes,
into tumbled gray spaces
where crooked sheep float.
Light takes shape in the rusted arms
of the dredge—a cathedral setting
where my husband walks, part symphony,
part dancing bear. Maybe it's the finale.
I stand up and clap just in case.

He closes his book.
"You were asleep," he says.
"Yes. I was asleep." I remember
he is preparing for his New Life,
looks sadly at mountains.
"It rained," he says, "I thought it would."
If I put on my blue dress he won't notice
if I leave by the window—
I'm kneeling on the sill when he kisses my neck,
"I won't forget you in my New Life," he says.
We dance around the room, bumping into things.
The cracks on the ceiling go out, one by one.

Lydia Vizcaya/Duck Valley Reservation

Where Scuffed Rocks Edge the Road

Tough, torn cobwebs tie my building
to a door, which doesn't close, it creaks.
Mule-eared dog wanders by
knows more of what goes on here than I
who listen and watch the loneliness
to see this place when no people are here.
My face will take the sun,
and if stiff-legged as the blistered door,
I can stay
shoulder like a wall, retaining songs
of a woman laughing past sorrow.

Norman Weinstein/Boise

Winnemucca, Nevada

coyote told bear-child:

this is where the White Devils
believed they found
entrance to the bowels
of the earth/Note

how the layout
of the city most
resembles a human
anus prepared
to expel gas. & how
its citizens are mainly
gas &
water held together
by this fiction they call
"tourist bucks." Don't

you find
this concept
of place rather
bizarre, bear-child?

                      bear-child
scratched its furry head
& replied:

Not at all, coyote
brother. I have heard
in the White Devil's
Scripture that when

Apocalypse comes
thousands of citizens
will flee California
& arrive, panting, credit
cards in hand at these
motels & filling stations

eventually, they will
find the accomodations
wanting & build cities
underground

coming into the dusty air
once a year
for a rodeo or
funeral or

a trip to the bank

A Place in Place of Father

In Idaho he didn't fall,
this honey-gatherer
from a tree. He fell

in Long Beach, too-old
from not enough honey
savored. Resurrected by 3

sons, not his: *Hear-It-However
Faint-the Sound; Follow-It-However
Great-The-Distance; Put-It-Together*

However-Small-The-Pieces.
How can his word-gatherer
son in Idaho fields ask the

fathers of hearing following
seeing which life worth
telling gives that father-

ghost final rest? Listen.
Crow's microtones awaken
the too-old father to just

old enough. Blink. There's
a path under childhood's
last hill. Let eyes draw

limbs as honey pours. Span
of a left hand coheres
this forest. These three

voices—layer upon layer—
echo as the honey jars
scraped from out of that

falling chorus a harmony
—dead father's voice inside mine—
buzzes & from a tree a branch

splits
—not savior—
savor of knowing place.

FAY WRIGHT/COEUR D'ALENE

A Window Provides the World

with the pattern of screens, crosshatched
memories defined like the blue enamel cup
handed up through the light. Carefully
blown upon and sipped, this coffee,
these two people, given and received in surprise,
like the *chrrring* of waxwings come back

for spring. Nothing keeps
from being given away—not bread or love
or water spilling over. Everything opens
and falls to somewhere downhill.

Summer windows are washed and the smell
of vinegar prompts the cat to heat.
More kittens will spill out of boxes
dribbling sour milk in the sun. They
will learn to pounce on milkweed and
roll in peppermint, while the woman will
have dreams like prayer wheels to sleep on
and wake fitful about the garden, the grave
mounds of potato and corn. Moths will begin
to beat against the late night windows.

By autumn the screens will be full
of papered wings and anthers
pieces of flight caught in a honeyed mesh.
The man will gaze out through his collection of dream—
bleached moths, furred eyes—looking back
to the heap of yellow locust leaves he played in.
He will fan his woolen arms,
an amazed bee in a dangerous hive.

In the morning
steam will begin to collect on the window
as a man and a woman rise from between heavy blankets
to a fire made of cedar
and the knowledge that winter,
like a good shadow,
requires a talent for holding still.

Christina

Bird-like ankles crossed,
a hip
cupping dry air,
you are a horizontal scarecrow
with nothing to protect
caught,
on the mute space of canvas.

But you hold mysteries
braced on a bony arm
held by the thrust of a narrow back
alerted to the flap
of any black bird's wing.

And thus pinned to a thin horizon,
it seems you've found a way
to give
without
being given away.

ROBERT WRIGLEY/LEWISTON

The Sinking of Clay City

When the last mine closed
and its timbers turned pliable as treesap,
the town began to tilt, to slide
back into its past like a wave.

Old men, caught by the musk
of seeping gas, arrived at the mineshafts
hours before dawn. Their soft hands
turned the air like handles on new picks.

Here and there a house split,
a cracked wishbone,
and another disappeared like crawlspace
behind a landslide.

So the townspeople descended the sloping entrances,
found them filled with a green
noxious water. Each drank a little
and forgot about the sun.

Some dug at rusted beercans
or poked at a drowned rat, more patient
than dedicated archaeologists,
and waited for their other lives to join them.

Fireflies

Now there are no fireflies. Once
there were, and we caught them.
Children, our white sweaters glinting
in the dusk, chasing after other children.
They seemed that way, children
or the very old, dottering in slow flight.
We'd charge any flash and wait
at arms' length for one another. And always,
there was. Once we kept them
in an unwashed honey jar, three dozen
snagged and flickering on the oozy sides.
Carefully we plucked each away and wrote
with the smear of their phosphorescence
our names on a stone wall,
and afterward licked our fingers,
and they were sweet and golden.

Heart Attack

Throwing his small, blond son
into the air, he begins to feel it,
a slow-motion quivering, some part
broken loose and throbbing with its own pulse,
like the cock's involuntary leaping
toward whatever shadow looms in front.

It is below his left shoulder blade,
a blip regular as radar, and he thinks of wings
and flight, his son's straight soar and fall
out of and into his high-held hands.
He is amused by the quick change
on the boy's little face: from the joy

of release and catch, to the near terror
at apex. It is the same with every throw.
And every throw comes without
his knowing. Nor his son's. Again
and again, the rise and fall, like breathing,
again the joy and fear, squeal and laughter,

until the world becomes a swarm of shapes
around him, and his arms
go leaden and prickled, and he knows
the sound is no longer laughter
but wheezing, knows he holds his son
in his arms and has not let him fly

upward for many long moments now.
He is on his knees, as his son stands,
supporting him, the look on the child's face
something the man has seen before:
not fear, not joy, not even misunderstanding,
but the quick knowledge sons

must come to, at some age
when everything else is put aside—
the knowledge of death, the stench
of mortality—that fraction of an instant
even a child can know, when
his father does not mean to leave, but goes.

The Drunkard's Path

Under the drum-taut top and backing I knelt
and needles pierced the muslin sky
like fireflies or lightning. There,
my mother's legs, her feet bare,
shoes abandoned behind her. I knew
somehow she was young that day.
Back and forth she shifted her feet,
easy on the cool linoleum floor.
The others, old women in heavy black
shoes, hosiery rolled to just
above the knees, here and there
the blue-gray slip of flesh, sickly
in the quilted light, and the great
encompassing stillness, how never
in that barn-hollow church basement
chamber of echoes did any feet move
but my mother's.
                    Today I have awakened
underneath that quilt again—underneath it

in sleep and in dream, the dream fading,
linoleum giving way to mattress, hard
coldness bleeding into warmth.
I move my feet outward, away
from where they have been, to find
again the coolest corner of the sheets.
I trace with one finger the known
and intricate pattern and look
at ceiling, staggered,
where sun through an open window plays
off the dew, and above me slivers of light
weave and flicker, and drunkenly flash.

HARALD WYNDHAM/POCATELLO

Entering the Water

Go slow.
It will look like nothing if you hurry.

Set your gear down on a rock, let the line
drift off on its own.

Look into the water.
How it sluices under the low branches
where the small trout scoot up and hang in the half-
    shadow,

how it washes the colored stones, yellow and red, flecked
with orange, black, quartz and mica, banded
from sediment, silica, sandstone,

or tumbles over the amputated stumps of aspens toppled
years ago by beaver to be wedged together
and packed mud-solid backing up green water ten feet
    deep

the white cascading curtain
roils the big hole where white and blue-green water
spreads out to the dark brown edges, ledges of yellow
    stone, mud,

or lips and trips downstream over boulders and lava-rocks
in a stair-step of rapid water where trout
flicker from stone to stone, orange tails—

how dark green with leaves and debris settled out it curls
against a huge rock carving it slowly, the stone
gnarled as an old man's skull, water

makes its own music on three levels, preludes
easily missed until the thunder

of that continual churning hammers through sense
and you become water, body and mind

broken, penetrated, overwhelmed, swept off and drowned
beyond time, neither living nor dead,

calm as a curled leaf riding the uneven water.

Swimming in Silence/Drowning in Light

Sunlight enters
             the white skull of the sheep
through sockets open to air
                  my skull
should be that empty
             shot full of
pure sunlight

&

the stream rushes
    RUSHES!
how long has it been pummelling?

carving these black canyon walls
washing soft silt down the mountain

&

waterwashed pebble
round as an opal
what can you tell me?

darkveined traveller
from the earth's center
what will you give me?

thoughts are dust
wisdom crumbles like dust

&

i am young
                    (i am nothing)

nothing gathers in me
but light crashing through like water
thunders it away

&

anger the need to kick
things to shout and shake

i want to be among trees
to lie in long grass
beside unspeaking rocks

&

water has been rushing all the time I was
writing these words
                    for days before I came here
and for years before I was born
                            (i who am so
young on the earth)
                    nothing can hold
that much water
                    (RUSHING! RUSHING!)
mountains of melted snow

&

when I am among people
the deep longing to wander far away
comes over me like a music made of water

&

at the top of the footpath up the mountain
light falls simply onto the broken shale

&

I have been alive twelve thousand mornings
my heart has pulsed over one billion times

(to what purpose?—to bring me here)

&

the longer i am silent
the closer i become

Graveshift in the Humping Yard

Midnight—
moonlight ices the reefers.

Early June, but cold enough
the pin-puller on the hump keeps his hands
tucked under his arms, waiting for
a deuce or trey.

Down the bowl the cars drift quiet as death,
moving toward you like an iron fist
to slam KAWHUMPH! into the waiting train.

When the boys in the towers muff one,
you have to drag that cut-of-cars back through the
retarders, making the metal-to-metal squeal
like whales singing in the night.

By five a.m. the skyline's black on blue.
Light sifts into the east above the warehouses.
The boys ride back in the cab of the yard engine,
swinging their lanterns as they drop off at the shack.

Stop in at the Whitman for a beer and a bite to eat.
Pocatello, Idaho—working for Uncle Pete.

Seed Store

The dry, pungent odor of nitrogen fertilizers,
peat moss, potting soils and dry beans in a barrel
mingles with the varnished fragrance of bamboo rakes,
brand-new shovels, wicker bowls and baskets
and something else I could never put my finger on.
Twenty colors of speckled seeds under glass
in wooden boxes with metal scoops buried to the
hilt in dehydrated abundance of hybrid corn
make up the magic of this amazing store.
And the proprietor, a sober gent,
with a straw hat and goat-skin gloves,
thin as a beanpole with a puritan preacher's face,
tends to the needs of lady gardeners, keeping
a weather-eye open for small boys who wander
among the red clay flowerpots and white crocks,
enchanted by green ceramic frogs.
If the roof ever leaked, the entire store
would be alive with tendrils and stalks, daffodils
in display cases and ivy climbing the walls.
Even today in memory, the place is GREEN,
and the owner, thumbs hooked in his brown apron,
stands rooted, like a beansprout, in the front doorway.